Fun & Collectible Kitchen Towels

Fun & Collectible Kitchen Towels
1930s-1960s

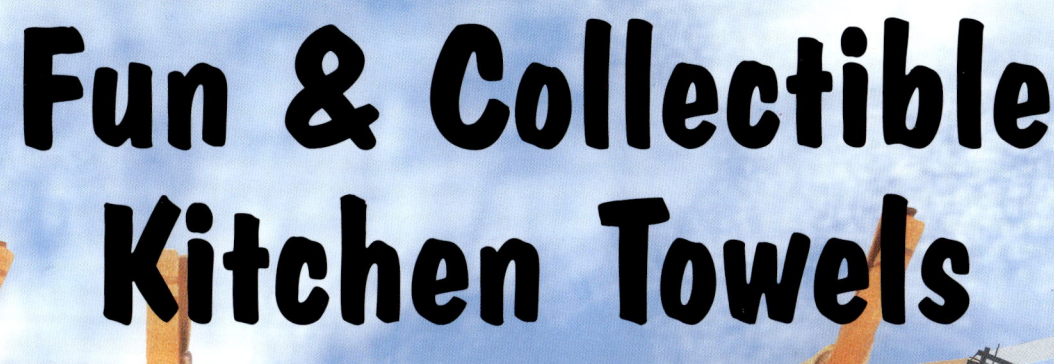

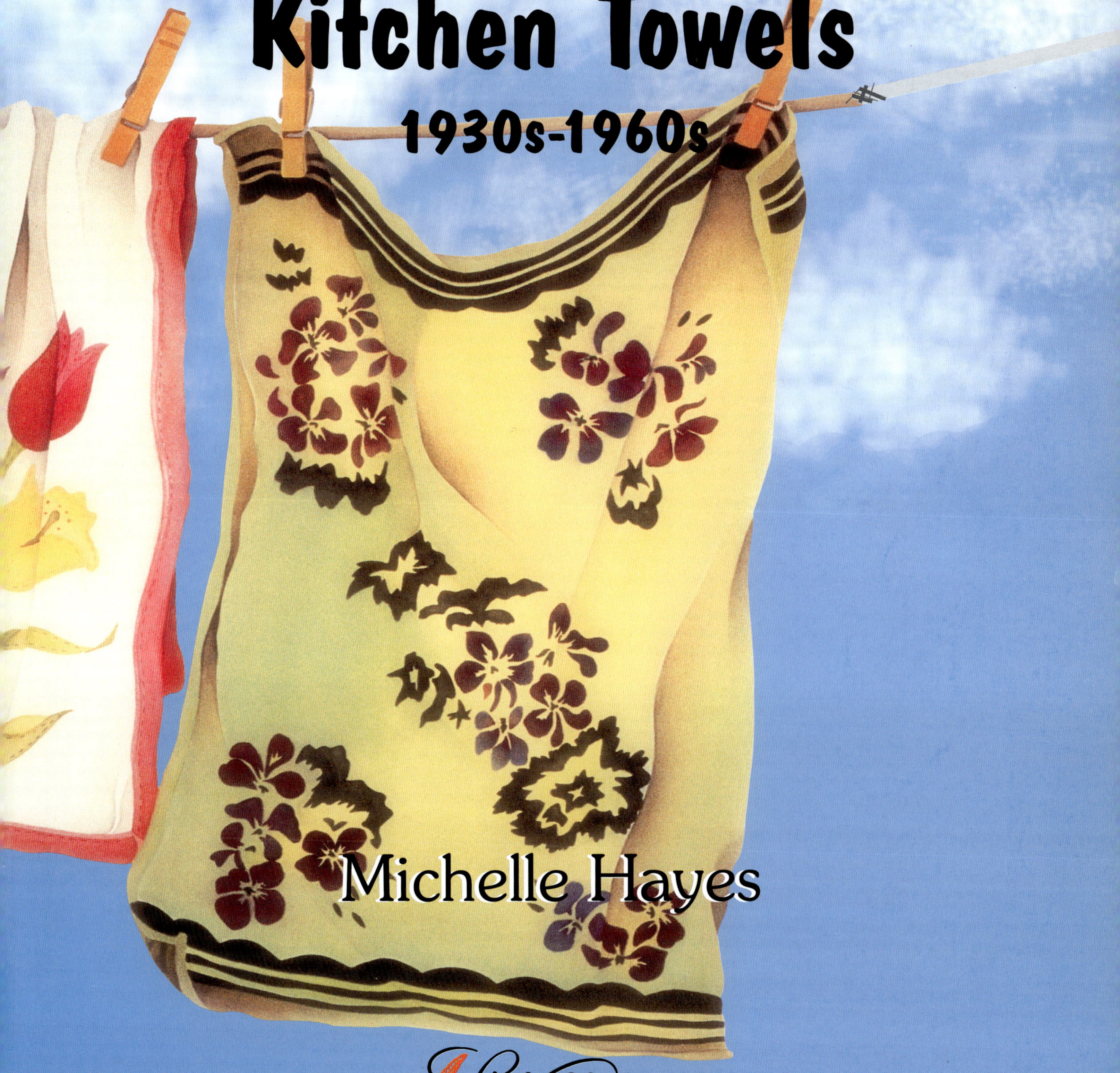

Michelle Hayes

Schiffer Publishing Ltd

4880 Lower Valley Road, Atglen, PA 19310 USA

Acknowledgments

I wish to thank the following people for their kind assistance: Joseph Sultan, Sultan Linens; Luther Travis, artist; Charles Haddad, Haddad Apparel; Carol Paulsen, artist; Susie Seymour; Shannon Stipes, Linda Hall Library; Fallani & Cohn; Elaine Reed, Plaid Enterprises; Karen Humphries, Tom Mathews, Springs Industries; and Gretchen Bingle, Kay Dee Designs.

Title Page

"Dishtowels," by Carol Paulsen. ©1998 Carol Paulsen/Rights International Group. Aaron Ashley Inc., Yonkers, NY

Copyright © 2005 by Michelle Hayes
Library of Congress Control Number: 2005930047

All rights reserved. No part of this work may be reproduced or used in any form or by any means—graphic, electronic, or mechanical, including photocopying or information storage and retrieval systems—without written permission from the publisher.

The scanning, uploading and distribution of this book or any part thereof via the Internet or via any other means without the permission of the publisher is illegal and punishable by law. Please purchase only authorized editions and do not participate in or encourage the electronic piracy of copyrighted materials.

"Schiffer," "Schiffer Publishing Ltd. & Design," and the "Design of pen and ink well" are registered trademarks of Schiffer Publishing Ltd.

Designed by Mark David Bowyer
Type set in Dom Bold BT / Souvenir Lt BT

ISBN: 0-7643-2315-6
Printed in China
1 2 3 4

Published by Schiffer Publishing Ltd.
4880 Lower Valley Road
Atglen, PA 19310
Phone: (610) 593-1777; Fax: (610) 593-2002
E-mail: Info@schifferbooks.com

For the largest selection of fine reference books on this and related subjects, please visit our web site at
www.schifferbooks.com
We are always looking for people to write books on new and related subjects. If you have an idea for a book please contact us at the above address.

This book may be purchased from the publisher.
Include $3.95 for shipping.
Please try your bookstore first.
You may write for a free catalog.

In Europe, Schiffer books are distributed by
Bushwood Books
6 Marksbury Ave.
Kew Gardens
Surrey TW9 4JF England
Phone: 44 (0) 20 8392-8585; Fax: 44 (0) 20 8392-9876
E-mail: info@bushwoodbooks.co.uk
Free postage in the U.K., Europe; air mail at cost.

Contents

Towel Manufacturers 6
    Martex 8
    Westpoint Stevens 12
    Spartan Textile Mills / Startex 13
    Weil & Durrsé 14
    Bucilla — Bernhard Ulmann & Co. 15
    Fallani & Cohn 18
    Cannon 19
    Hadson 24
    Springmaid 25

Food 26
    Chefs 26
    Fruits and Vegetables 38
    Southwest and Mexican 52
    Poultry, Meats, and Seafood 54
    Vera 64
    Desserts 65
    Beverages 69
    Calories 80

Outdoors 83
    Farm Scenes 83
    Christmas 90
    Florals 93
    Birds 104
    Cats and Dogs 107
    Scottish Terriers 111

People 112
    Garden Girls 113
    Dancers 123
    Servants 128
    Wedded Bliss 135

Childhood 141
    Children 141
    Nursery Rhymes 146
    Circus 148

Bath Sets & Pillows 150
Cleaning and Storage 153
Glossary 156
Bibliography 159
Index 160

Towel Manufacturers

Montgomery Ward 1943 catalog page, "Printed Towels...useful and decorative."

The Office of Price Administration (OPA) was a U. S. federal agency established in the World War II era to prevent wartime inflation. In April of 1942, the OPA issued a general maximum price regulation that made prices charged in March of 1942 the ceiling price for most commodities. The OPA succeeded in keeping consumer prices relatively stable during the remaining war years. Besides controlling prices, the OPA was also empowered to ration scarce consumer goods in wartime. Tires, automobiles, sugar, gasoline, fuel oil, coffee, meats, and processed foods were ultimately rationed. At the end of the war, rationing was abandoned and price controls were gradually abolished. The agency was finally disbanded in 1947. Price tags with an OPA price can date an item to a selling date between 1942 and 1947.

Floral display showing pinks, daisies and roses. An all around border of pansies and roses. The price tag from Sears, Roebuck and Co. remains affixed, showing an OPA price of .39 cents. G W Prismacolor. Manufacturer: Grossman & Weissman. Inc. New York. Price range: $18

G W Prismacolor tag. Sears, Roebuck and Co. price tag with OPA price.

Martex

This is a gift set for the bride and consists of five striped linen towels measuring 17 x 34 inches each. Wrapped nicely with a ribbon that has the "Martex" name imprinted on it. The descriptive paper label reads "Martex Bridal Gift" and shows a picture of a smiling bride. Manufacturer: Martex. Price range: $25

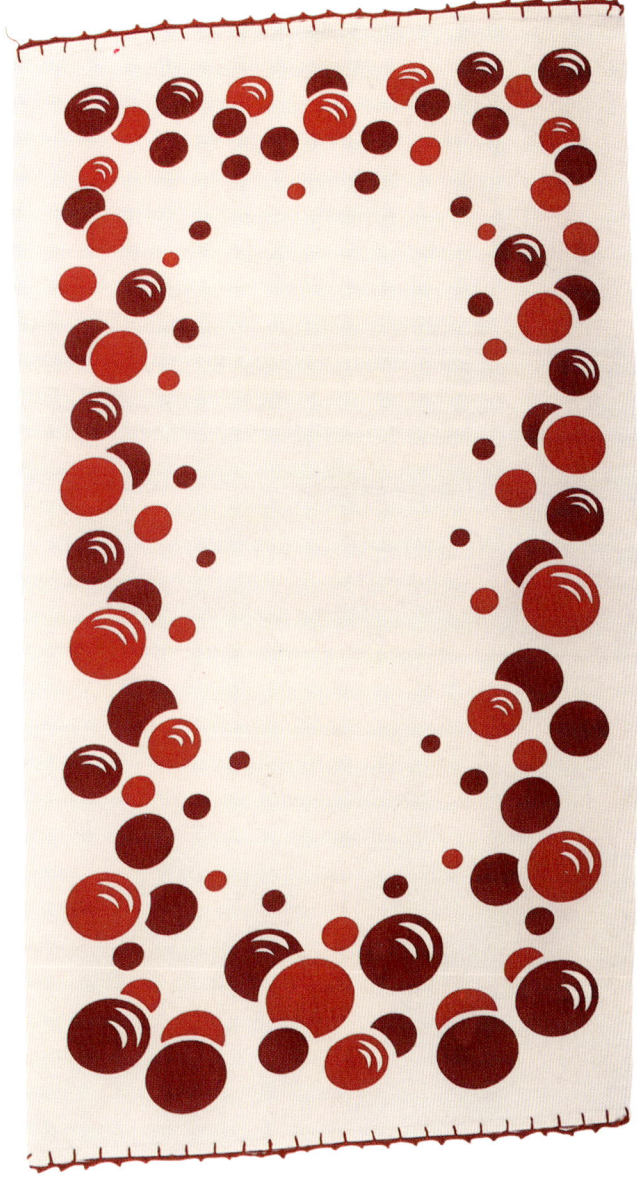

Art Deco towel with a floating bubbles design in red and burgundy. Has a sewn in Martex Dry-Me-Dry tag. Price range: $15

The Martex Company was founded in 1914 by William H. Margerison and Albert Ernest Margerison. They originally produced Turkish towels, terry-cloths, bath rugs and washcloths. In the late 1920's, Martex was purchased by West Point Manufacturing company.

Mammy and child stirring up a cauldron of soup. "Too many cooks spoil the broth". Martex. Artist: Ann Orr. Price range: $20

Martex tag

Magazine advertisement for Martex bubbles towel. June, 1937 *Good Housekeeping* magazine.

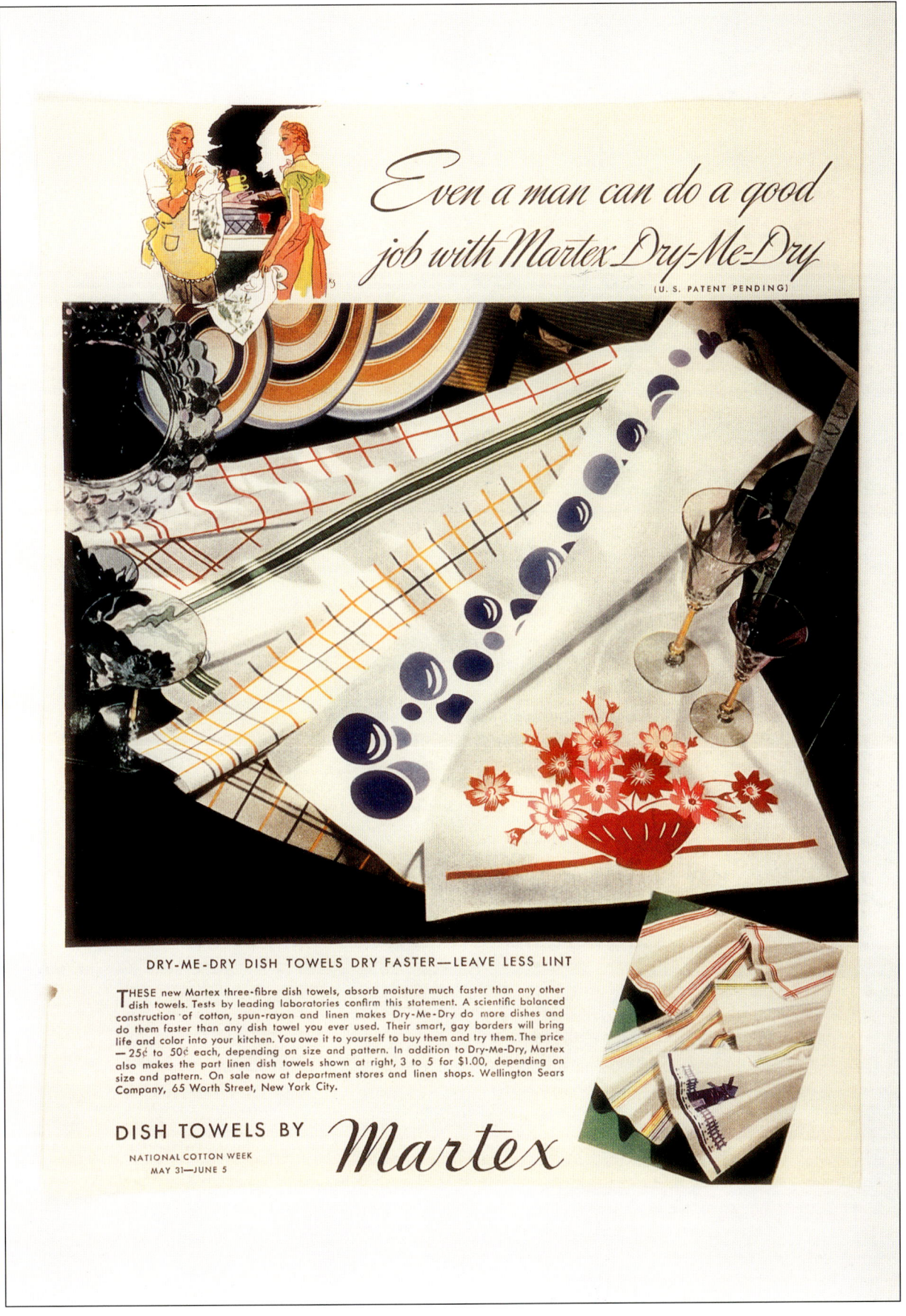

Late 1930s magazine advertisement for Martex towels. This ad shows a husband and wife sharing the dish washing chores using Martex kitchen towels. Many of the Martex advertisements and labels would show this picture along with the statement "Even a man can do a good job with Martex Dry-Me-Dry." The ad states that the price for the Dry-Me-Dry towels shown are priced from 25 to 50 cents each and the standard towels in lower corner are priced at 3 to 5 for 1.00.

 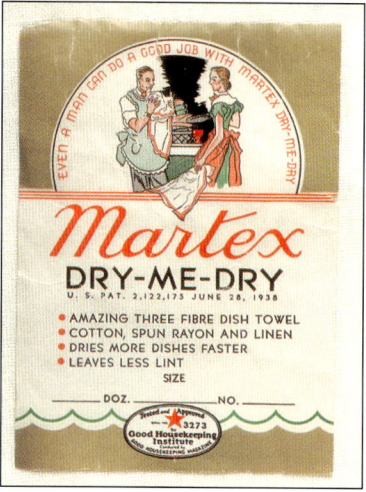 

Martex standard dish towel label. Their standard towels were fabricated of a cotton and linen blend and measured 17 x 34 inches. They were advertised as a "reliable and speedy dryer."

Martex Dry-Me-Dry towel label. The Dry-Me-Dry towels were described as "amazing three-fibre dish towel." These were fabricated from a blend of cotton, spun rayon and linen. This Dry-Me-Dry blend was patented by the inventor, Charles P. Coulter, Jr., in 1938.

An Ann Orr design showing a gentleman carrying a basket of vegetables with a plump pig at his side. "To market to market to buy a fat pig." Martex. Artist: Ann Orr. Price range: $20

WestPoint Stevens

J. P. Stevens towel commemorating 40 years of business. The towel states "Stevens Fabrics Famous For 40 Years 1899-1939." Each corner shows a different fiber: a cotton boll for cotton, a lamb held with a ribbon and bow for wool, flax flowers for linen, and a hand holding a beaker for rayon. This is a wonderful historical towel for the Stevens Company made specifically for their annual sales dinner in 1939. Price range: $75 *From the private collection of Karen Humphries*

Wedding Anniversaries. This towel lists the gifts that are given for each anniversary from the first through the fifteenth and then every five years until the 60th anniversary. Pink bows, ribbons and roses decorate the sides and make a flowery display to the words "Wedding Anniversaries." White cherubic angels with arrows and blue tinged wings in center. This retains the original manufacturer's sticker from "Stevens Linen Assoc. Inc." Price range: $15

WestPoint Stevens is a conglomeration of three of the oldest and most successful companies in American textiles. These three companies were:

J.P. Stevens & Co., founded in 1813 by Nathaniel Stevens.

Pepperell Manufacturing Company, founded by Samuel Batchelder. In 1844, Pepperell Manufacturing Company's first cloth mill was built on the lower bluff of the Saco River, in Biddeford, Maine.

Westpoint Manufacturing Company, founded by Lafayette Lanier shortly after the Civil War, in West Point, Georgia.

Each remained an independent company until 1965, when West Point and Pepperell merged to form WestPoint Pepperell. In 1993, WestPoint Pepperell acquired J.P. Stevens, in the final step to create the WestPoint Stevens company.

Spartan Textile Mills/Startex

Startex Curt-Towel in the Jewel Tea "Autumn Leaf" design. These towels were called "Curt-towel" because they could also be used for curtains and were sold with large hems for that reason. The label reads "Kitchen Towel with a double use. The attractive kitchen towel for the fastidious home-maker. 2 towels will also make a pair of decorative kitchen curtains. Insert rod through hem and hang." They were sized 20 x 35. Jewel Tea started out in 1899 as a tea, coffee and spice business. As a reward for shopping with Jewel Tea, customers could collect free dinnerware based on the amount of their purchase. The dinnerware offered was the Autumn Leaf design made by Hall China Company. Manufacturer: Spartan Mills. Price range: Set of two with paper tag $60. Set of two without paper tag $40.

Tea cups, teapots and creamers all lined up in orderly parade fashion with tea pots and coffee pots as their leaders. Bordered all around in red with the words "Kitchen Parade." Each item carries a fork or spoon and they all have smiling faces. Startex called these "Sack Towels." The 1956 Sears Midwinter catalog describes these towels as "Printed Sacking Squares" in Jumbo size. "Ideal for dishtowels...for clever café curtains, aprons, table covers. Order several for an inexpensive and different kitchen ensemble." These were priced at two for 67 cents. These were also sold in the 1956 Montgomery Ward Spring and Summer catalog and were described as "The traditional pots and pans pattern in singing colors and daring design for a cheerful kitchen." They were priced at three for $1.09. Startex. Manufacturer: Spartan Mills. Price range: $15

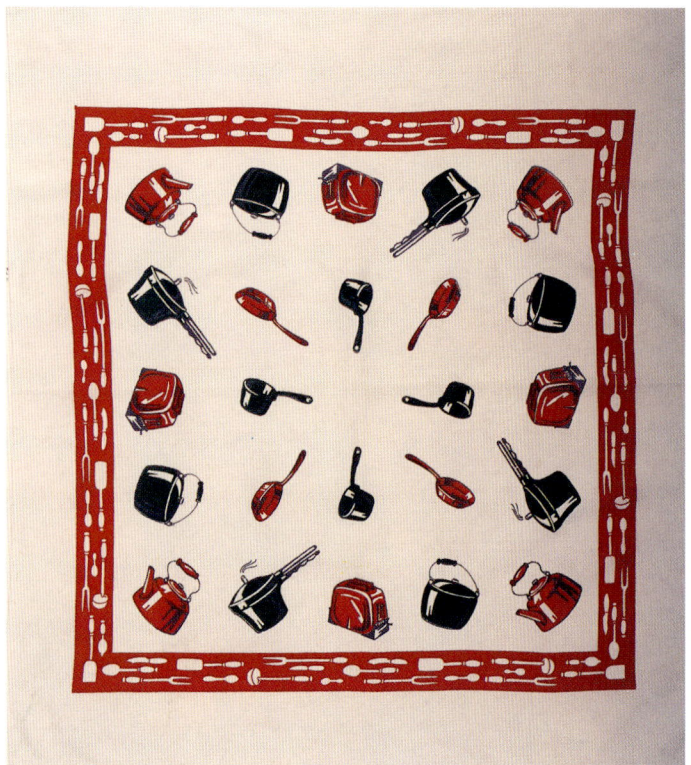

Towel by Startex showing pots, pans, teapots and kettles in bright green and red in an all over pattern. Manufacturer: Spartan Mills. Price range: $15

Startex advertisement for their crash toweling. "Has linen spun and woven both ways." *The Ladies Home Journal*, January 1922.

Spartan Mills was founded in 1890 in Spartanburg County, South Carolina, by John Montgomery. The company began by producing ropes, bags and cotton bats and soon after, cotton sheeting, bag goods and broadcloth. In 1902, John fell to his death from scaffolding at a new plant in Georgia and his son Walter became president. Walter was a leader in the new field of human relations for textile workers and worked to make life better for the mountain people who worked at the mill. He built a hospital for the 2,000 Spartan Mill workers and in 1907, he built the "Textile Industrial Institute" junior college to encourage better educational opportunities for his employees.

Walter died in an auto accident in 1929 and his son, Walter S. Montgomery, took over and ran the company for the next 44 years. After World War II Spartan expanded, purchased other mills, built new ones, and was known for high quality cotton household fabrics under the brand name "Startex," which is a familiar brand name to vintage textile collectors today. Economic recession and increasing world market competition caused Spartan Mills to close in 2002, after 112 years in business.

Weil & Durrsé

The Weil & Durrsé Company was founded by Leopold Weil and Jacob Durrsé. The company produced tablecloths, towels, napkins, curtains, bedspreads, toweling, and piece goods under several brand names, including Wilendur, Wilendure, America's Pride, and Pride of Flanders. Their textiles were produced in many different fabrics, including cotton sailcloth, Belgium linen, and a cotton/rayon blend. In the 1950s Jacob Durrsé's son, Jacob G. Durrsé, took over the company with his partners, John Goodman and Alex Guralnick. Mr. Durrsé closed the Weil & Durrsé company in 1984 to enjoy his retirement years. Weil & Durrsé linens are very popular with vintage linen collectors, and are known for their beautiful and brilliantly colored printed designs on high quality fabrics.

Flower pots on the windowsill with red shutters and ruffled curtains. Note the brightly colored flower pots and the heart-shaped cutouts on the wooden shutters. Manufacturer: Weil & Durrsé. Price range: $20

Pot of begonias with ceramic pig planter done in a floral design. Manufacturer: Weil & Durrsé. Price range: $20

Bucilla - Bernhard Ulmann Co.

Bucilla was founded in 1867 by Bernhard Ulmann, a European emigrant. Mr. Ulmann originally sold napkins, doilies and handkerchiefs printed with silk-screened embroidery designs from a push-cart on the streets of east New York. In 1870, he opened his first and only retail store; in 1875, he began to sell his products to other retailers. The company was first known as Bernhard Ulmann Company, Inc. (Lace, Linen, and Accessories) and was shortened to Bucilla, an acronym of the longer name. Bucilla provided high-quality yarns and supplies for knitting, needlepoint, and embroidery and became a well-known publisher of books and patterns related to needlework. Instructional books on various needlework methods, knitting, and pattern books were enormously popular and helped Bucilla become a common household name. Bucilla was owned and managed by the Ulmann family until 1922, when it was sold to its employees. The employee-owned company flourished until 1962, when it was sold to Indian Head Corporation, a well-known conglomerate of the time. Indian Head was purchased by Hannson Trust, a Swedish company, in 1966. Hannson owned Bucilla until 1977, when it was sold to Armour-Dial, a division of Greyhound Corporation. Bucilla changed hands once again in

Weil & Durrsé towel paper tags.

1983, when it was purchased from Armour-Dial by a group of private investors. Its success continued, and in 1996, the company was purchased by the Dyson-Kissner-Moran Corporation and placed under the direction of Plaid Enterprises, where it remains today.

Bucilla paper tags.

Apple pie. The recipe for apple pie is written around the border of this towel. The farmer holds a hayfork and the lady dances with a pie in her hand. The name "A. Farmer" is printed on the yellow mailbox. Manufacturer: Bucilla. Price range: $15

"Plum pudding." The recipe for plum pudding is written around the border. The gentleman dances in the background while he carries a bucket of beer suds and the smiling lady proudly holds a tray with plum pudding. A white lamb with a red bow around her neck prances along, and the yellow puppy pulls the lady's shoestring. Manufacturer: Bucilla. Price range: $15

Home sweet home. Grandfather sits in his rocking chair, reading and smoking a pipe. Note his red striped sock and the elaborate pattern on his chair. Kitty is curled up asleep and Grandmother carries a steaming covered dish. Around the border it says "Mid pleasures and palaces through I may roam – Be it ever so humble there's no place like home." Manufacturer: Bucilla. Price range: $15

Turkey in the straw. Happy dancing children with haystacks and turkeys. Around the border it says "Turkey in the hay roll em up a high tuckahaw and hit em up a tune called turkey in the straw." Manufacturer: Bucilla. Price range: $15

Bucilla tag

Fallani & Cohn

The Fallani and Cohn company was founded in the 1920's by Tom Cohn Sr. and remains a thriving textile business today. They produce tablecloths, towels, napkins, placemats and related kitchen textile accessories. Although the company is no longer owned by the Cohn family it retains the Fallani & Cohn name. Their vintage tablecloths and towels are very popular today and can still be found in many designs. They have produced linens under several brand names including Hearthside, Falspun, Falfax, Nantucket, and State Pride Kitchen Companions. Hearthside is the only line they still use. Luther Travis, Tammis Keefe, Rosemary Newson, Peg Thomas, Martin and Lorraine Ryan (The Ryans), Doris Duffee, and Pat Meyers are just a few of the artists who have designed linens for Fallani & Cohn. Some years ago, the artist Pat Meyers designed a children's Melamine dishware set with matching placemats for Fallani & Cohn. Fallani & Cohn has produced household linens for companies such as Nikko and Marimekko, using those companies' designs, and they currently produce linens for Waverly, Woolrich, and Royal Doulton, among others.

1964 advertisement with towels, styled by Luther Travis for Fallini & Cohn.

Yellow and white striped cat surrounded by assorted cheeses and two little mice watching her sleep. Artist: Doris Duffee. Manufacturer: Fallani & Cohn. Price range: $15

Cannon, Cannon/Fieldcrest, Cannon/Pillowtex

Cannon Mills was founded in Concord, North Carolina, by industrialist James William Cannon in 1887; by 1898 he produced the first cotton hand towel manufactured in the South. The demand for Cannon Towels grew so rapidly that in 1905, Cannon bought a 600-acre farm about seven miles from his original plant. Here he built a new towel mill and started the village of Kannapolis (the name is of Greek origin, meaning "loom city"). Under the guidance of James Cannon's son, Charles, Cannon Mills became the world's largest producer of household textiles, including sheets, towels, and bedspreads. Cannon became a household name around the world.

In 1982, Financier David Murdoch took over Cannon Mills and merged the company, in 1985, with Fieldcrest Mills Inc., making Fieldcrest Cannon a world leader in household textiles. Fieldcrest Mills had been founded in 1893, in what is now Eden, North Carolina.

The Pillowtex Corporation was founded in 1954, in Dallas, Texas. In 1997, Fieldcrest Cannon was purchased by the Pillowtex Corporation, but retained the Fieldcrest Cannon name. The 116 year history of Cannon Mills entered a new era in 2003, when Pillowtex closed down their business. The Cannon textile mills in Kannapolis, North Carolina, which once made more household textiles than any other plant in the world, were shut down, and the city became the center of the largest layoff in North Carolina history. The consortium Official Pillowtex LLC acquired the assets of the Pillowtex Corporation, including the Cannon and Fieldcrest names. Later, Li & Fung USA was licensed to use the Cannon name, so although the Kannapolis Cannon textile mills are no more, the Cannon name continues.

Cannon was the first to develop towel styling which set the pace for bathrooms and kitchen design. Color became a dominating factor in home decoration and Cannon introduced towels in pastel colors. In 1928, Cannon introduced "towel ensembles" consisting of bath towels, face towels, wash cloths and bath mats in matching sets.

In 1929, Cannon held the first Towel Style Show ever conducted.

Cannon was the first to print four-color product catalogues, the first to sew actual brand logos into textiles, and the first to market designs derived from Hollywood films.

This gift towel set by Cannon includes one towel and one wash cloth. Appealing design of kittens wearing blue bows sitting in a wood cask surrounded by flowers. Still enclosed in this set is the gift card which reads, "to Mary and Bessie from Aunt Mary 1955." Price range: $25

These small 2 x 3 inch boxes would hold a 14 x 24 inch towel, as shown here. Box reads "Inside this box is a gift for you…New Style, Candy-Striped."

Striped kitchen toweling. Cotton linen blend measuring 17 x 68 inches. Shown in the 1943 catalog page to the left. Price range: $22

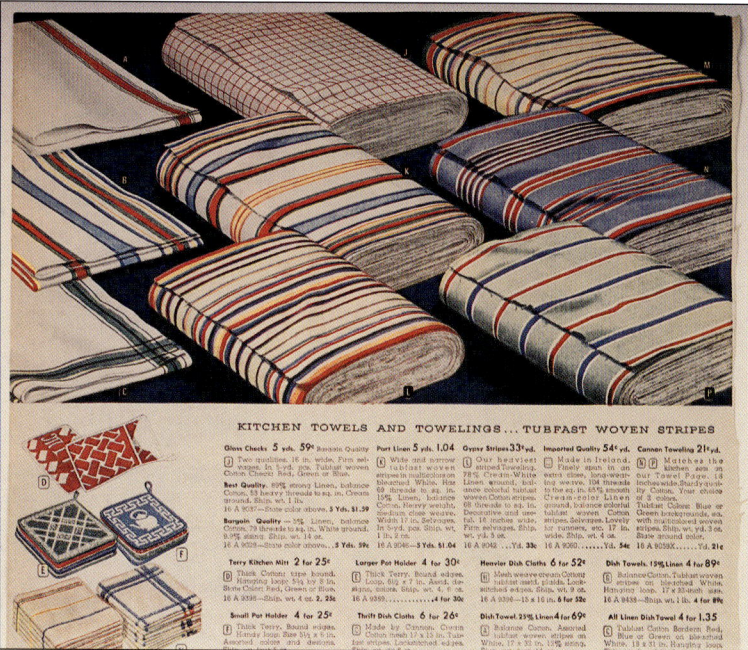

Montgomery Ward 1943 catalog page showing bolts of striped kitchen toweling. The striped towel is described "Cream-color linen ground, balance colorful tub-fast woven cotton stripes. Lovely for runners, etc." 17 in. wide and priced at 54 cents a yard.

Charming design on terrycloth with red and white striped hat box with ribbon, pump spray perfume bottle, red fan and two clip-on pearl earrings. Lower part of towel shows tube of red lipstick, pearl necklace, powder puff tied with red ribbon, small jar of red rouge, and a beautiful glass perfume bottle with cut glass stopper. Background of polka dots and lip prints in red. Price range: $18

Throughout the years, kitchen and bathroom towels have been advertised in catalogs and magazines. One of the more interesting advertising series was by Cannon, during World War II, for bath towels depicting military life. They show American soldiers enjoying a brief time of fun and relaxation amid the terror of war. Cannon based these advertisements on letters written to them by servicemen. Notice that an advertisement was produced for each branch of military service.

"Alaskan Aquacade." True Towel Tales: No. 2…in a letter from a flier in Alaska. Illustration from description in flier's letter. Soldiers bathing with buckets of icy cold water.

"Army Day – Crocodiles Keep Out!" True Towel Tales: No. 1. Told by a doctor in the medical corps. Illustration as described by the Army Medico. Soldiers cooling off in the South Pacific Islands.

"What? No Bath Salts?" True Towel Tales: No. 3…As told by a U.S. Marine. Illustration from photograph supplied by U.S. Marine Corps. Marines using a primitive water tank for showering in the Solomon Islands.

"Tank Corps." True Towel Tales: No. 4…as told by a sergeant in the tank corps. As illustrated by the sergeant. Soldiers enjoying a welcome swim as a relief from the Mediterranean heat, fight-fatigue and pestering flies.

"Hey, Turn Off The Water, Jumbo!" True Towel Tales: No. 5…As told by a sailor. Illustration as described by the sailor. Sailors receiving a shower-bath from an elephant in Colombo, Ceylon.

"Buna Bathtub." True Towel Tales: No 6…as told by a soldier. Illustration as described by the soldier. "We came across this Buna village," says a private in the Army, "and down on the beach was a canoe that the natives had no use for. It was full of rainwater and we were dirty. The natives thought we were wacky — but watta bath, brother, *watta* bath!"

The Lever Brothers Company included a Cannon dishtowel in their boxes of "Silver Dust" laundry detergent.

Along with the boxed towel, Silver Dust included a small pamphlet, which gave ideas for making useful articles with the dish towels.

Inside the Silver Dust pamphlet. "It's Easy! And you will enjoy making the different articles pictured in this book. Attractive for kitchen or bathroom are curtains and valance made of three dish towels. It takes two dish towels and three yards bias binding to make this useful laundry bag. From five dish towels, make a good-looking luncheon set: 1 runner; 4 mats; 4 napkins. For your home, for bridge and bingo prizes, for church and lodge bazaars." The pamphlet also advertises their towels as wonderful for gift giving. "Pack 6 Silver Dust towels in any gay gift box, tie it up with a pretty bit of ribbon and you'll have a prize or present that will delight the heart of any woman."

23

Advertisement for Breeze detergent showing Cannon kitchen towel. The ad reads, "Inside every giant economy size box of new all purpose Breeze is a big Cannon Dish Towel worth 25 cents. Large size box contains Cannon Face Cloth."

Hadson/ Carolina Manufacturing

Hadson stood for Haddad and Sons. Saul Haddad was the father and the sons were Eli, Sam, Morris, and Abraham. The original business began as a fancy goods store located at 50 Allen Street in New York City, founded in 1920 by the eldest brother, Eli Haddad, and his father, Saul Haddad. They later sold silk underwear in 1925 and in 1933 moved to 518 Broadway, New York City, where they sold linens. They moved once again, to 313 Fifth Avenue, New York City, in 1935.

They eventually sold imported clothing, umbrellas, dishes and ceramics, household linens including tablecloths and towels, as well as Japanese and Belgian rugs. They also sold battery and wheel-operated toys made in Japan, at one time being the largest in the business. These were all made under the brand name *Hadson*. One can still find these items with the *Made in Japan* stamp on the bottom of the toys, dishware and figurines, and stated on their paper-tagged linens, all showing the Hadson logo, an anchor.

The company name, which originated in the 1930s, was Carolina Mfg. Co. The name came about because they were manufacturing bedspreads in North Carolina. During World War II, sheets and pillow cases were manufactured in Passaic, New Jersey and sold to catalogue companies such as Sears Roebuck and J.C. Penney. In 1947, they were one of the first companies to go to Japan to buy merchandise. Originally they purchased stock lots of Japanese merchandise. One very large purchase was all kinds of clothing that were made for the Japanese army. These items were sold to the five and dime stores such as McCrory's, S.H. Kress, H.L. Green, J.J. Newberry, F.W. Woolworth, and S.S. Kresge. These stores no longer exist today.

Hadson was one of the largest general merchandise importers in 1948. As the years moved on they were selling jewelry; lighters; men's, ladies' and children's gloves; footwear; toys; crockery; dinner sets; rugs; transistor radios; lace goods; and men's, ladies' and children's apparel of all kinds.

Now known as Haddad Brands, they deal only in licensed boys' and girls' apparel, accessories, hosiery, and footwear. Some of the famous brands that they are currently selling are: Nike, Levi's, Harley-Davidson, Dickies, Major League Baseball, and Michael Jordan. The company remains in the Haddad family and is currently operated by Charles S. Haddad, Chairman; Edward S. Haddad, CEO; Charles A. Haddad, V.P.; and four sons.

This is a humorous/sad motif towel. One side shows a plate, teapot, fork, spoon and vegetables crying while the other side shows the same characters with happy smiling faces. Note the tears dripping from their faces and their little square hands rubbing their eyes. Hadson. Manufacturer: Carolina Mfg. Price range: $18

Springmaid

Labels used with permission of Springs Industries.

Springmaid toweling fabric manufactured by Springs Mills. Springs Mills was founded in 1887 as Fort Mill Manufacturing Company in Fort Mill, South Carolina by Samuel Elliott White. Leroy Springs established Lancaster Cotton Mills in Lancaster, South Carolina in 1895 and in 1914 his company assumed control of the Fort Mill Manufacturing Company. By the early 1900s Springs Mills owned five textile mills in South Carolina: Fort Mill Plant, White Plant, Lancaster Plant, Kershaw Plant and Eureka Plant. Their Springmaid linens show their logo, a maiden holding a water jug at the water mill. Springs Mills, now called Springs Industries, remains in business today selling all manner of household textiles including sheets, pillowcases, towels, window blinds and shades, decorative pillows, bedding ensembles, home sewing fabrics, bed and bath products for institutional and hospitality customers, apparel products, and rugs and accessories. Springs Industries remains a private company still owned by the Springs family and led by company Chairman Crandall Bowles, a 5th generation member of the Springs family.

Springmaid towel.

Food

Chefs

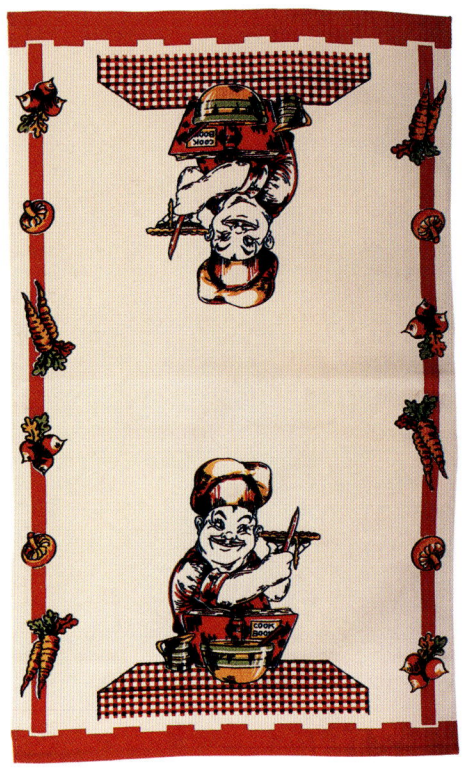

Impish, mustached chef trims a pie crust, with his cook book, bowl, and sifter on the table. Vegetables line the sides. Price range: $18

French chef with black mustache and a blue kerchief tied around his neck. Red and white checked shirt and chef's hat. Note the green ladle and pot cover and the red accents to the chef's face. Progress Creation. Manufacturer: Tobin, Sporn and Glaser. Price range: $18

Portly chefs with steaming cups of coffee and cherry pie. The floral plates have scalloped edges and the scene includes forks, spoons and rolling pins. Startex. Manufacturer: Spartan Mills. Price range: $15

This happy chef is licking his chops as he watches the unsuspecting vegetables and fish walk toward the soup pot. Artist: Tom Lamb. Price range: $22

Chef holding a plate with a pheasant resting on it. Table with tablecloth, bowls of fruit, wine carafe and wine glass. Price range: $15

Pastry chef carries fancy decorated three-layer cake and holds a stack of bowls. A broken teapot with a surprised look on its face lays on the carpet. He wears wide red and white checked chefs pants and a floral shirt. Note the purple accents on his face and his black mustache. Broderie Creations. Manufacturer: A. R. Rosenthal & Co. Inc. Price range: $20

Chef playing an instrument which appears to be a beet, while little smiling vegetables dance around him. Broderie Creations. Manufacturer: A. R. Rosenthal & Co. Inc. Price range: $25

This is a comical design showing chefs and animals in a cooking theme. The chef holds a platter of meat while he dances with a pig. A cow wearing a tuxedo, red bow and black top hat imbibes a bit of wine with the chef. Towel still retains the sticker "Hand Printed Pure Linen By Leacock." Manufacturer: Leacock and Company. Price range: $18

Chef Willie with kitchen utensils and fork and spoon design. Willie Thall was an emcee for the show "Midwestern Hayride," which was a popular 1950's-60's television show broadcast from WLW in Cinncinnati, Ohio. Price range: $15

Package of Vogart transfer patterns showing the many different Chef patterns included and ideas on how to use them such as towels, toaster covers and pot holders. This set of patterns is called "The French Chef – Man of Kitchen Distinction – in a Dozen Poses." "Gay and colorful, their humorous approach to culinary chores is guaranteed to transform any kitchen ensemble." These hot-iron patterns were simple to use. The design was cut out, placed on the textile and pinned and then ironed with a quick stroke of a medium hot iron. Purchase thread in the colors shown on the package front, hand embroider and the housewife has a charming towel to bring smiles and style to her kitchen. Manufacturer: Vogart.

Hand embroidered design showing a chef flipping pancakes and a steaming cup of coffee by his side. An iron-on Vogart transfer pattern was used for this towel. Manufacturer: Vogart Crafts Corporation, New York. Manufacturered craft and hobby kits and sets, transfer patterns, artists paint tubes and accessories, needlecraft frames, linens and pre-cut fabrics stamped for embroidery, iron-on transfers, embroidery floss and all manner of crafting accessories for needlework. Vogart was purchased by the large needlework company, Bucilla, and is now owned by Plaid Enterprises. There are no current products under the Vogart name. Price range: $18

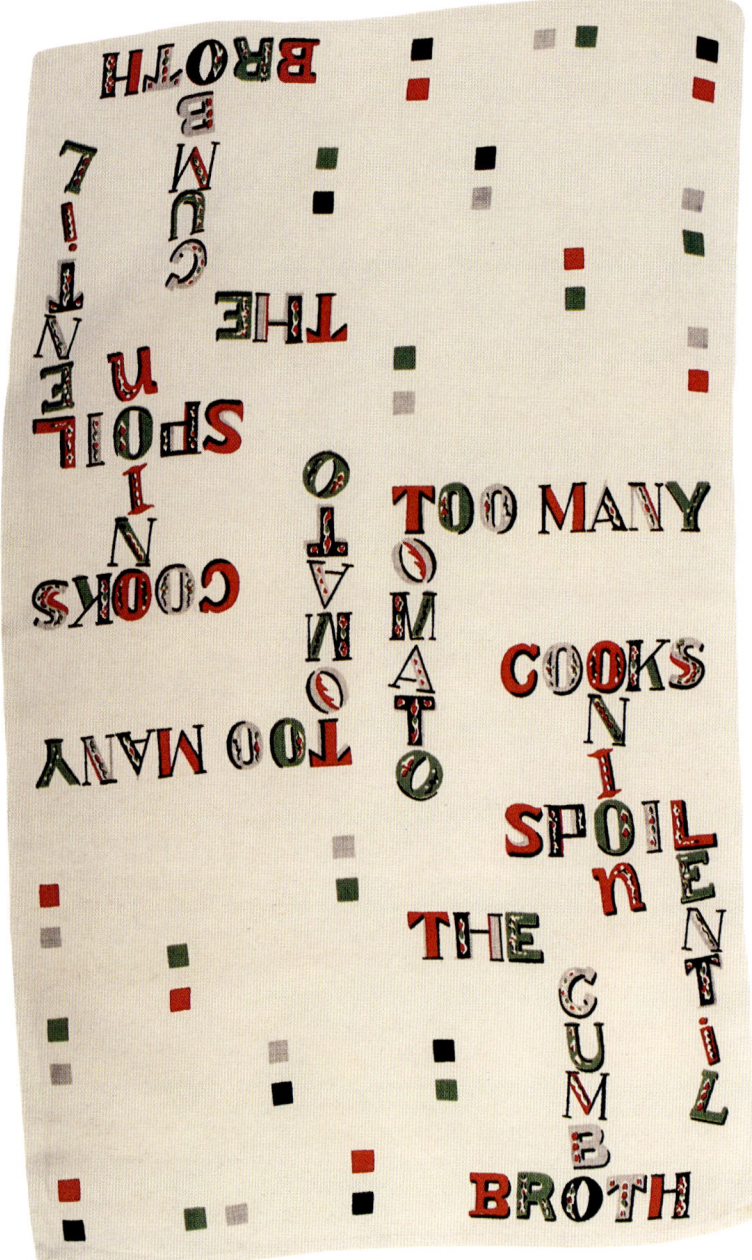

This towel shows multi-colored letters spelling out "too many cooks spoil the broth." Additional letters are added to form the words "Tomato, Onion, Lentil, Gumbo." Price range: $15

Housemaid and chef so mesmerized by each other that they fail to see the soup pot boiling over on the stove. Manufacturer: P & S. Price range: $15

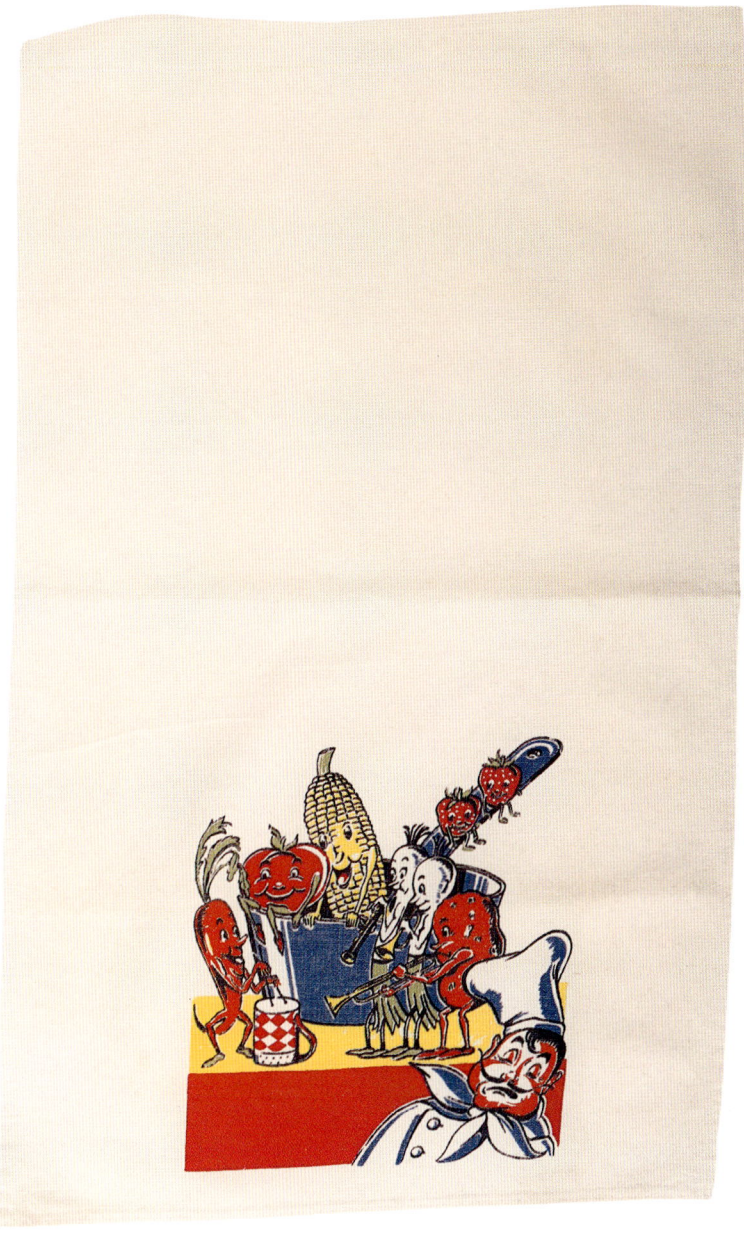

Cheerful chef with names and pictures of various herbs such as garlic and thyme. A banner with a poem which reads "Stews and Salad taste twice as nice when flavored with some herbs and spice." Manufacturer: Leacock and Company. Price range: $15

Random House Dictionary describes anthropomorphic as "resembling or made to resemble a human form." The expression often used is simply "people like." This towel is a perfect example of an anthropomorphic design, with the vegetables having human-like faces and, going a step further, wearing shoes and skirts and have apparently even formed their own musical ensemble! Note the sleepy chef in the corner. Price range: $15

Colorful chef with oversized fork and tea pot at his sides. On his tray is a bird and cherries, and small birds chirp in the corners of the cloth. Note the chef's apron and his red hat with white polka dots. Broderie Creations. Manufacturer: A. R. Rosenthal & Co. Inc. Price range: $22

Very colorful and detailed towel shows three men cooking in the kitchen on one end with the other end showing three women cooking. The men roll out pastry dough and flip pancakes, and the women prepare a piecrust. Note the different colors of the women's shoes and see how their hair is blonde with black accents. The sides are decorated with teapots, ladles, sieves, cutters, butter dishes and more. Towel still retains the "fast color made in Japan" sticker. Hadson. Manufacturer: Carolina Mfg. Price range: $18

Broderie tag

Waiter holding a menu and a tray with a smiling teapot. Sugar bowls on tables and pottery on shelves all have little faces. Broderie Creations. Manufacturer: A. R. Rosenthal & Co. Inc. Price range: $22

Mammy. Smiling mammy stirs a pot of soup while little girl looks on. Peas in their pods, tomatoes, celery and milk on the table, with sugar and salt displayed on the shelf. The shelf has a scalloped border and is decorated with cherries. Little girl has many red bows in her hair, and the mammy wears a colorful red floral dress with yellow apron. Price range: $25

Black mammy wearing kerchief and floral apron holds a steaming hot pie. Price range: $25

Black mammy holding a plate with a stack of pancakes and flipping up some more. Stacks of pancakes, knife and fork, and coffee pots line the sides. Note her yellow slippers and her matching skirt, bandana and head kerchief. Startex. Manufacturer: Spartan Mills. Price range: $25

"What's Cooking." Hot dogs roasted over the campfire with onions and mustard decorating the sides. Large black fork holds the pink hot dog. Original Town House Kitchen Decoratives. Artist: Lois Long, artist, illustrator, and textile designer, was born in Clarksdale, Mississippi, in 1918. She studied design and later taught at Pratt Institute in New York. She wrote and illustrated the *Mud Book* with her friend, John Cage, and also illustrated the *Mushroom Book* with Cage. Manufacturer: Hedaya Brothers. Price range: $15

"What's Cooking." French-cut potatoes being fried in a pot, and peeled and unpeeled potatoes line the sides. Note the yellow-handled knife and potato peeler. This retains the fabric content sticker that reads "All Pure Linen Made in Ireland." Price range: $15

"What's Cooking." Another design in the What's Cooking series. This one shows pasta in a pot with mushrooms and garlic, and a bottle of Chianti. Artist: Lois Long. Original Town House Kitchen Decoratives. Manufacturer: Hedaya Bros. Price range: $15

Poem on cooking written in a mixture of German and English. Grandmother is making a pie and she says "um it gifs pot pie" and "ach such wittles." The sides are decorated with pictures of loaves of bread, plates of turkey, cup of steaming coffee, and doughnuts. Price range: $15

Fancily clad lady seasons the dish while a concerned chef looks on. "Too Many Cooks Spoil The Broth!" Buckets of ice, martini shakers and even tiny hibachis line the sides. Price range: $15

Progress Creation towel paper tags.

Breakfast, Luncheon, Dinner towel. A dancing chef with Scottie dog, girl with tray of dishes, whistling teapot on the stove and a couple sitting down to dinner. Dishes, silverware and fruit decorate the sides. This retains the original "Progress Creation" sticker. Manufacturer: Tobin, Sporn & Glaser, Inc. New York, founded in 1895. They manufactured quilts; fabrics; household linens stamped for embroidery, drawn work, and art needlework; needlework items, including embroidery thread, floss, and yarn; bed and table covers; and printed kitchen linens. Their linens were produced under several brand names, including Progress, A Progress Creation, Progress Quilts, Styled By Tobin, and Tobin Home Fashions. Tobin, Sporn & Glaser, Inc., remained in the same family from 1895 until 1999. Donald Tobin, as president and owner, sold the company to Maytex mills in 1999. The Tobin Home Fashions name continues under the ownership of Tobin/Maytex, producing table linens, napkins, and placemats. Price range: $15

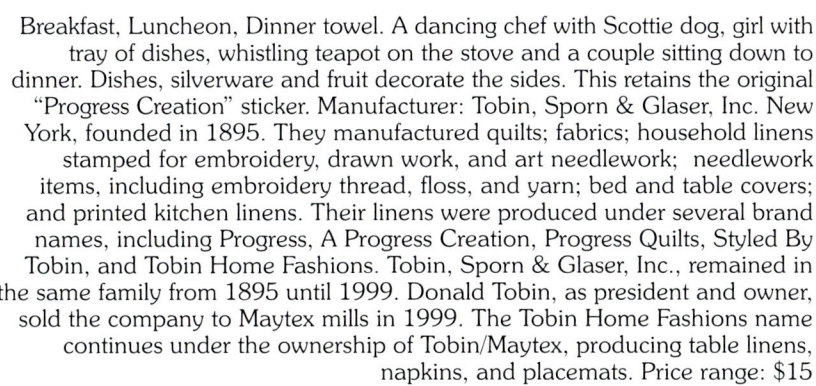

"Too many cooks spoil the broth." Three cooks wearing big white chefs hats and stirring up a concoction. Price range: $15

Fruits and Vegetables

Clusters of deep red strawberries and green leaves. Note the gold burnish to the blossoms. Manufacturer: Weil & Durrsé. Price range: $18

Grape leaves and clusters of burgundy grapes decorate the center with a black and white stenciled grape design on the sides. The pattern name for this is "Grape-Arbor." This design was sold in three colors: burgundy, gold, and purple, all with matching tablecloths. This is the first design Luther Travis did for Fallani & Cohn. Artist: Luther Travis. Manufacturer: Fallani & Cohn. Price range: $16

Luther Travis designed household linens from the 1950s through the late 1990s. He received a B.A. in interior design and fine arts from the College of William and Mary and studied textile design at Parsons School of Design in New York. He worked as a designer and art director for Bloomcraft for 31 years. Bloomcraft manufactured printed and woven decorator fabrics and sold matching ensembles such as bedspreads, curtains and linens. The items he designed for Bloomcraft in the middle to later years of his employment there have his signature which is shown in the selvage of the fabric. During this time he also worked as a free lance artist for several companies, including Town & Country Linens, Fallani & Cohn, and Hedaya Brothers. He free lanced as a textile designer for Fallani & Cohn for over 35 years, from 1960 to 1999, designing many kitchen linens. He designed linens for Hedaya Brothers under their Original Town House Kitchen Decoratives brand line from 1956 through 1960. Every item he designed for Fallani & Cohn, Town & Country Linens, and Hedaya Brothers has his signature on it. Each year he would design different Christmas linens for Fallani & Cohn and would also do spring designs usually showing flowers in light summer colors, and a fall design which would show fruits and autumn colors. Many of his designs were made into sets such as a tablecloth with a matching towel, potholder, toaster cover and apron. In the 1960's he designed several handkerchiefs for Sturbridge Village. He also designed an herb motif tablecloth for Sturbridge Village through Fallani & Cohn that was inspired from the Sturbridge herb garden. Mr. Travis designed Christmas cards for a company called American Artist Group. He did a line of 12 to 14 Christmas cards for them each year from 1965 until 1984. After he left Bloomcraft he went into business licensing himself to textile companies designing interior decorative products such as wallpaper with coordinating bed linens. Mr. Travis retired from the textile design business in the late 1990's and now devotes himself to raising orchids.

Advertisement for "Grape Arbor" textiles, styled by Luther Travis for Fallani & Cohn.

Twining vines of fruit with cherries and flowers along the sides. Price range: $15

This is 10 yards of printed kitchen toweling, 17 inches wide, which retains the Startex Mills paper tag. A fruit design with grapes, pears, apples and cherries. This fabric was sold in the Montgomery Wards 1947-1948 Fall and Winter catalog, and was described as a "Startex colored fruit cluster pattern on white background. Woven from strong cotton yarn, serviceable, absorbent. For roller or dish towels." It was priced at 29 cents a yard or five yards for $1.39. Price range: $50

Cornucopias containing strawberries and flowers. This towel retains the original store price tag from J C Penney Co. and was priced at 10 cents. Manufacturer: Cannon Mills. Price range: $15

Red cherries with blue blossoms. Manufacturer: Cannon Mills. Price range: $19

Apples, cherries, grapes and pear on a plate with scalloped edges and floral design. Sides are lined with raspberries and blue cherries. Price range: $15

This bib was fabricated from toweling fabric with a blue apple and red leaf design. It was made for a very special occasion.

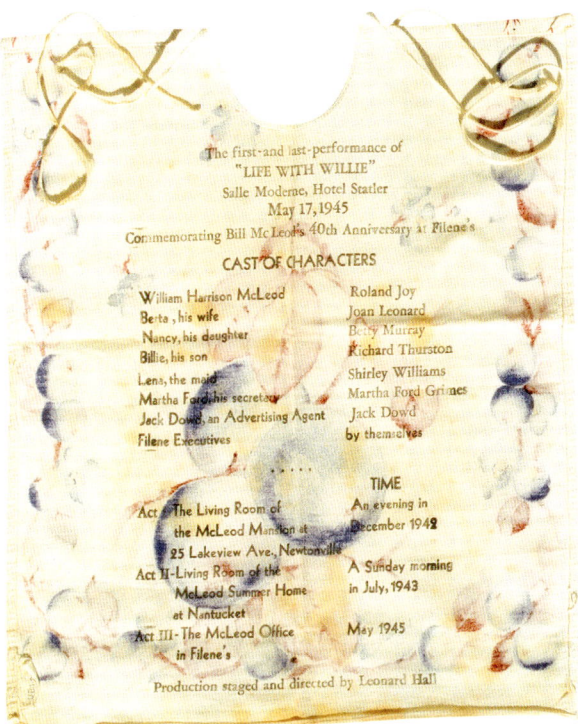

The back of the bib shows how unique it is as it was used as an announcement and invitation for a play celebrating William Harrison McLeod's 40th anniversary at Filene's department store. Filene's is an historic New England retailer in business for nearly 150 years. The bib reads "Commemorating Bill McLeod's 40th Anniversary at Filene's" and "The first and last performance of "Life with Willie" Salle Moderne, Hotel Statler, May 17, 1945." This is a wonderful piece of textile history and a novel use of toweling fabric.

Straw basket full of fruit. Strawberries and raspberries line the sides and apples decorate the corners. The basket handle has a blue ribbon tied into a bow, and the table is covered with a blue floral tablecloth. Price range: $15

Fruit and floral display with strawberries, cherries and branches of red and blue hollyhocks. Sprigs of raspberries and cherries are tied with blue bows, and fruit and flowers line the sides. This fabric was cut off the bolt in a two-towel width, and measures 32 inches wide x 27 inches in length. The housewife could purchase however many towels desired, in one piece, and with just a little cutting and hemming she had beautiful towels for her kitchen. Price range: $20

"Strawberry." Blue and red strawberries scattered in the center with a floral border. Shown sold in Montgomery Wards catalog. Price range: $15

"Cherry." Large branches of cherries with a white scroll border. Shown sold in Montgomery Wards catalog. Price range: $15

These towels were sold in the 1945 Montgomery Ward catalog. "Cheery placemats, gay towels and toweling." The strawberry toweling is shown as (15) and described as "Strawberry. Closely woven durable cotton toweling. Add a splash of color to your kitchen with matching scarfs, curtains and towels. 18 inches wide. Yard 53 cents." The Cherry toweling is shown as (14) and described as "Cherry dish towel. Two sprays of cherry branches against a white background accented by a flowing scroll border. Sanforized cotton. 16 x 28 inches. Each 50 cents."

Vegetable and fruit display with pumpkins and peeled bananas. Tiny vegetables line the sides. Price range: $15

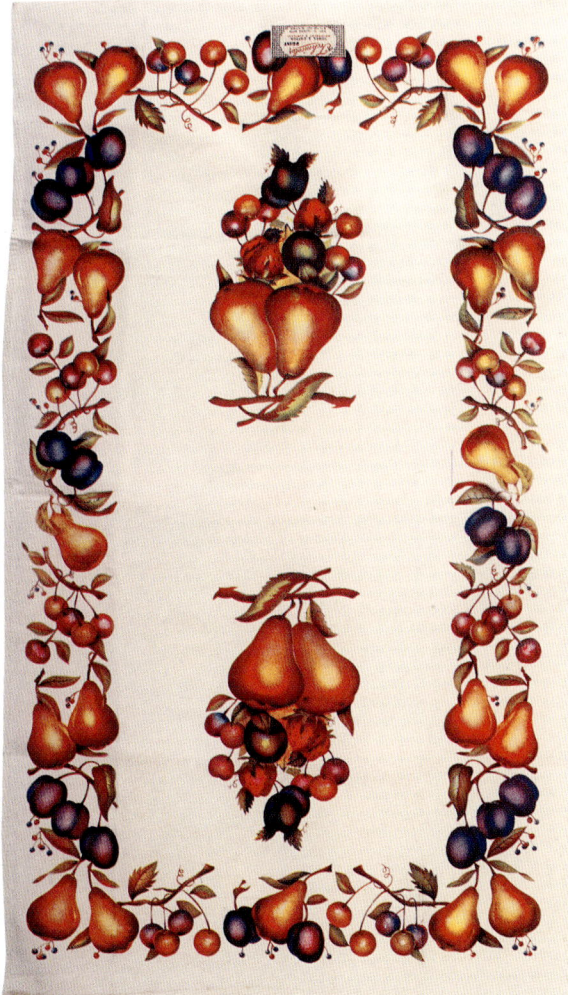

Cluster of fruits, including pears, cherries, plums and strawberries. All-around border of mixed fruits. Note the stunning gold burnish to all the fruits. A Technicolor Print. Manufacturer: Eaton. Price range: $15

Technicolor tag

Blue basket overflowing with strawberries and tied with a red ribbon. Reads "Hollywood Calif." Price range: $15

Appealing design showing blue water jugs and little blue baskets of strawberries. Bows and ribbons decorated with white daisies and strawberries swirl throughout the design. This is unused cotton fabric, cut from the bolt, measuring 16 inches wide x 11 feet in length. Price range: $55

Romantically pretty pink cherry design. Black and white striped bow and cluster of pink cherries in the center with the words "Cherry Pink." Note the unique border on one end with the edge cut in the shape of the cherries. Horse and carriage figure in corner of towel. Manufacturer: Town and Country Linen Corporation. Price range: $18

Martex Kitchen Garden paper tag

Weave basket with pineapple, beets, tomatoes and more spilling out. Vegetables line the sides. Note the green floral tablecloth on the table. Hadson. Manufacturer: Carolina Mfg. Price range: $15

Two towels from a series of vegetable design towels produced by Martex called "Kitchen Garden Collection." Black tinged white onions with green leaves on a mustard colored background. Original price tag from "E. W. Edwards & Son" attached and priced at three for 99 cents. Second towel has a stark black background with yellow ears of corn. Yellow diamond-shaped corn holders. Original price tag from "Sibley, Lindsay & Curr Co." attached and priced at 49 cents. Their tags read "A new group of contemporary designs and colorings in famous Martex "Dry-Me-Dry" (cotton-rayon-linen) construction." They have sewn-in labels stating "The Amazing 3 Fibre Towel, cotton-rayon-linen". Manufacturer: West Point Textiles. Price range: $15 each

Another in the Martex "Kitchen Garden Collection" this one with big red radishes down the center and the sides decorated with sliced radishes. Original store price tag from "E. W. Edwards & Son" attached and priced at three for 99 cents. Price range: $15

Recipe for French dressing with salad bowl and vegetables all on a pink background. Detailed cut-glass salt and pepper shakers, and oil and vinegar decanters sitting in a silver tray. Note the fancy fringed curtain border. Price range: $18

Vegetable design with yellow and red vegetables lining the sides, and wood bushel baskets full of tomatoes in the corners. Pot and baskets connected by a string pull a harvest of radishes and tomatoes. Note how the artist has added connecting string and colorful wheels to the containers. Price range: $18

Unusual design in bright primary colors showing donkey and sheep planters in yellow with cactus, floral painted piggy bank, fruit bows and blue water jug. Of particular interest is the unusual character mug with a design of a woman on it. Price range: $15

Elves and cherries decorate this towel. The elves wear big chefs hats or striped stocking hats. Price range: $18

Broderie tag

Charming design with a donkey pulling a wagonload of smiling vegetables. The wagon is made with large round wheels and the donkey is painted aqua green. This towel retains the original store price tag that reads: "Frederick and Nelson, Seattle, 29 cents." Broderie Creations. Manufacturer: A. R. Rosenthal & Co. Inc. Price range: $22

Tomato and lettuce. Pin-up girl sitting on a pink wood fence with the words "tomato and" and shows a head of lettuce. Price range: $15

Pink tea pot with pineapple, grapes, cherries and apple. White floral border. Hadson. Manufacturer: Carolina Mfg. Price range: $15

This is a humorous/sad motif towel. One side shows a plate, teapot, fork, spoon and vegetables crying while the other side shows the same characters with happy smiling faces. Note the tears dripping from their faces and their little square hands rubbing their eyes. Manufacturer: Hadson. Price range: $18

Clusters of fruit and flowers in the center with a border of red fruit and leaves. This towel is shown on the following catalog page and priced at 27 cents a yard. Description reads "Fruit Cluster. Spice your kitchen with ripe red color. All cotton toweling of good serviceable quality to sew into kitchen ensembles." Width: 17 inches. Price range: $18

Montgomery Wards 1946 catalog showing toweling and towels. Their description reads "Toweling and towels at budget prices. Harmonized, gay with color, soft, sturdy, absorbent. Sew bright-as-sunshine kitchen ensembles … covers for chairs and table, cabinet and window curtains, mat sets … aprons for yourself!"

Southwest and Mexican

Western scene with lassoing cowboy on a horse. Cactus, saddle, frying pan with sizzling bacon border the ends of towel and belts with bullets decorate the sides. Price range: $18

Southwestern scene with colorful painted pottery, cactus, maracas and guitar. The sides are decorated with sombreros, scarves and gourds. Notice the multi-colored tiles done in soft water colors. G W Prismacolor. Manufacturer: Grossman & Weissman. Price range: $18

Young lady rolling dough in her kitchen and the walls and counters are lined with colorful pottery and gourds. Price range: $15

Southwestern patio scene with gray stone wall and red floor. Pottery in blue, yellow and red with dried corn and gourds hanging from a wall. Note the cloth with red roses and the wonderful mixture of colors and patterns on the rugs. Brilliantly rich coloring. Manufacturer: Weil and Durrsé. Price range: $18

A senor carries a bowl full of gourds with colorful pottery in the background. The sides are bordered with guitars, sombreros and gourds. Note his brightly colored hat and serape. Price range: $15

Pottery and gourds in cheerful colors with stripes, feathers and beads along the sides. Manufacturer: Weil & Durrsé. Price range: $18

Poultry, Meats, and Seafood

Prancing rooster in bright red and orange with flowers, hens and baby chicks in pink. Note the beautiful handwork of pink tatting the housewife added to this towel. Price range: $15

"Just between us girls." Pink hen sitting on a nest of eggs. Corn, silos and barns decorate the sides with baby chicks in pink, green and brown chirping on the ends. Price range: $15

"Just between us girls." Two hens gossiping over the garden gate with one mama holding her baby chick on her wing. A spade, hoe and water can decorate the sides. Price range: $15

Humorous scene with a rooster and a hen who appear to be a bit tipsy after imbibing their share of corn liquor. They are singing a happy tune of "cock a doodle doo chicken in a stew." Note their heavy lidded eyes and the "corn xxx" jug on the ground. Baby chicks decorate the sides. Price range: $15

"Chicken today feathers tomorrow." Old farm auto with a chicken driving and boxes of chickens in the back. Price range: $15

"Chicken today, Feathers tomorrow." Farm girl holds a black and pink rooster in her arms and roosters and chickens decorate the sides. Note her green pantaloons and braided green hair. Price range: $15

55

"Chicken today feathers tomorrow." Ma and Pa farmer dancing and drinking home made mash. In his gaiety Pa's glasses and hat fly off his head and he doesn't even care. Poultry dance a circle around the happy couple and a black man plays a banjo in the distance. Price range: $15

Mother carries a roasted turkey to the table while father and children wait. Note the plant with the smiling faces on the flowers. Father reads the newspaper and a Scottie dog keeps close to the turkey. Price range: $15

This lady with an unusual shape holds a fancy tray with dressed turkey. Old style keys dangle from her apron, her lips and the "roses" on her cheeks are blue, and she has a blue ribbon in her hair. Note the shape of the table legs. Price range: $22

This gift set from the 1960's combined towels in the always popular rooster design with wood salt and pepper shakers. Price range: $22

Rooster towels tied with red ribbons and a wood rolling pin painted in a bright Swedish floral design. Price range: $22

Colorful roosters on terry cloth. This set combines two towels with a ceramic deviled egg plate. Price range: $22

Funny duck towel with pictures describing a roast duck recipe. Shows little red duck, rub with salt and pepper, stuff with apples, roast one hour, turn, baste often. Note the yellow webbed feet of the duck, the fancy salt and pepper carrier, and the red ball handles on the roast pan. Price range: $18

Pork and beans. Yellow pig with yellow can of beans. Note the vine of red pods with black beans popping out and the yellow and red sausages along the sides. Price range: $15

Corned beef and cabbage. Bull and cabbage with mustard and horseradish. Price range: $15

Strongman lifting weights, and a wooden cutting board with a big slab of red meat. Pretzels, potatoes and a frothy mug of beer await consumption. "He-Man Food." Price range: $18

Steak and potatoes. Pink background with posies scattered around, with knives and forks along the sides. Note the necklace of flowers around the cow's neck. Price range: $15

Ham and eggs. Ham and eggs design showing two well-fed pigs and two eggs sizzling in the frying pan. Note the different colors of the pigs and the unusual design to the frying pan handle. Price range: $15

Bucilla sold towels stamped for embroidery and printed towels in the same designs. This shows three towels in the same design. One stamped and ready to embroider, one that has been embroidered, and one with the design in print. Manufacturer: Bucilla

Removing the potholder reveals a juicy pink ham.

This towel has a novel and useful idea with a potholder in the shape of a pig that snaps onto the towel. Apples, onions, mustard, and pepper grinder all in pinks and greens decorate the background. Notice the unusual design of pennies decorating the green stripe. Manufacturer: Paragon Needlecraft Corp., New York. Paragon Needlecraft was founded in 1929 and produced items for handwork, including crewel kits, needlepoint tapestry kits, needlecraft kits with stamped or printed fabric for embriodery, needlepoint, rug and quilt making. They also sold printed kitchen linens and finished kitchen linens with hand embroidered and appliqued designs, many of which were imported from China and the Canary Islands. Price range: $18

Ham and Eggs. Eggs in the frying pan and a farmer "hamming" it up. Price range: $15

This towel has the following sayings: "An apple a day keeps the doctor away" and "A pint's a pound the world around." A scale balances a pound of butter and a jug of whiskey, and fruits decorate the sides. Price range: $18

Colorful towel with tidbits of wise advice such as "penny wise pound foolish" and "waste not want not." A five-dollar bill with wings on it, red floral piggy bank with pennies and bread box with sliced bread. Price range: $18

63

Vera

Vera Neumann (1907-1993) became a well-known textile designer and artist from the late 1940s until her death in 1993. She designed the prints on many different household linens, including sheets, aprons, bedspreads, and cocktail napkins. Her tablecloths, towels, and scarves are popular again today, and often can be distinguished by her trademark "ladybug design" that she would draw next to her signature. Many of her designs show bright, oversized florals in wonderfully wild color combinations. One can still find Vera towels, printed on high quality linen fabric, in the vintage linen market with the original Vera paper sticker attached.

Vera tag

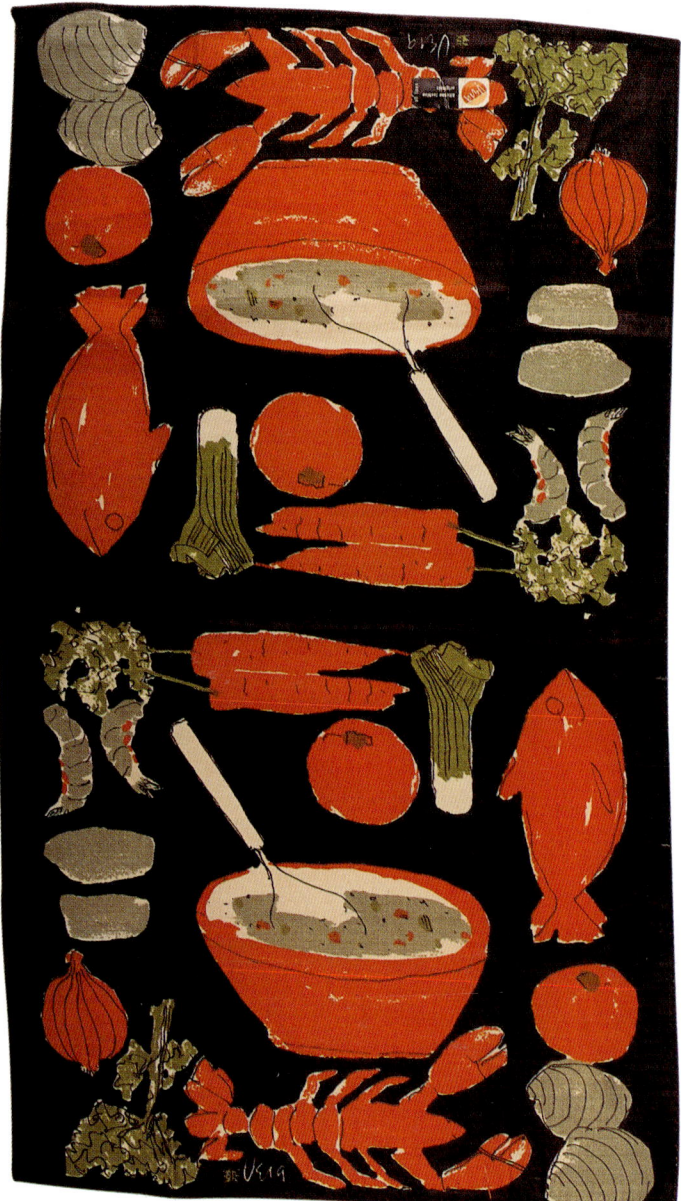

Vera design. Wonderful shish-ka-bob theme. Note the "swords" holding bell peppers, tomatoes, mushrooms and meat. The sides are decorated with glasses full of red wine. What a nice meal! This does not have the Vera signature or ladybug but does have a sewn in label on the hem that reads "Vera All Linen". Price range: $18

Towel designed by Vera. Seafood theme showing a soup pot of fish stew. The sides are decorated with all the ingredients necessary for a delicious fish stew including leeks, carrots, shrimp, fish, onions, oysters and more. A large red lobster decorates both ends. This has the Vera name and ladybug and also retains the "Vera all linens kitchen fashion originals" sticker. Price range: $18

Desserts

Salt cellar and flour holder with salt and pepper shakers and vegetable border. Price range: $15

Miscellaneous kitchen items such as steaming coffee pot, bowl of salad, coffee and tea canisters and cheese board with cheese. "The kitchen's best for all of these, where folks relax and eat in ease!" Manufacturer: Leacock and Company. Leacock and Company, New York, manufactured printed kitchen linens such as tablecloths and towels, and linens imported from Madeira with beautiful hand done embroidery and appliqué. They had several brand names including Leacock, Leaspun, Colfax and Quality Prints. Price range: $18

Ceramic flour container and jug with tear-drop shaped stopper. Spatulas in red and green, and clusters of berries. Price range: $18

65

Paint palette design with yellow and red flowers. Price range: $18

Sugar and spice. Decorative jars of candy and spices. Pots, knives, forks and spoons line the sides with black and yellow striped candy canes in center. Price range: $15

Large polka dot cookie jar on a red background. Cookies in different cut-out shapes such as shamrocks, stars and hearts. Price range: $15

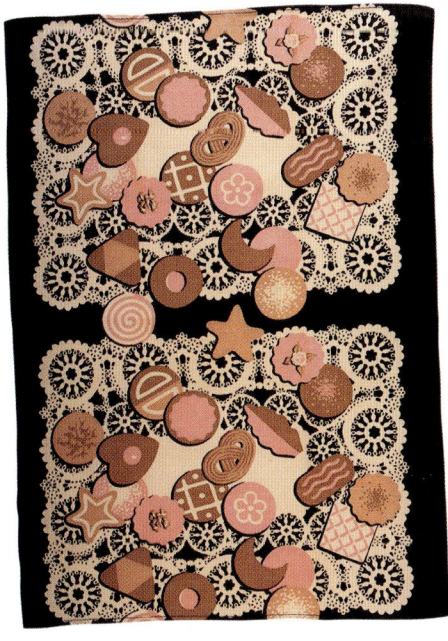

Cookie motif on a black background. Many different types of cookies in pink and tan on a white lace doily. Manufacturer: Martex. Price range: $15

Towel designed by Vera in an all-over pattern of candy. This has the ladybug mark and Vera signature. Price range: $15

Cupcakes, cupcakes, cupcakes! Entire towel covered with large cupcakes decorated with cherries, strawberries, frosting and swirls of whipped cream. Dramatic colors with black background and gray, pink, and red cupcakes. Price range: $15

Cuckoo clock, slice of cake, and strawberries spilling out of a box on a sunny yellow center with cherries and strawberries lining the sides. Price range: $15

Cheerful towel showing three happy little faces on sticks protruding from a plate of red aspic. Dessert dish with yellow concoction topped with cherry. Note the yellow caps on the faces and the blue with white polka dotted bows. Manufacturer: Bucilla. Price range: $18

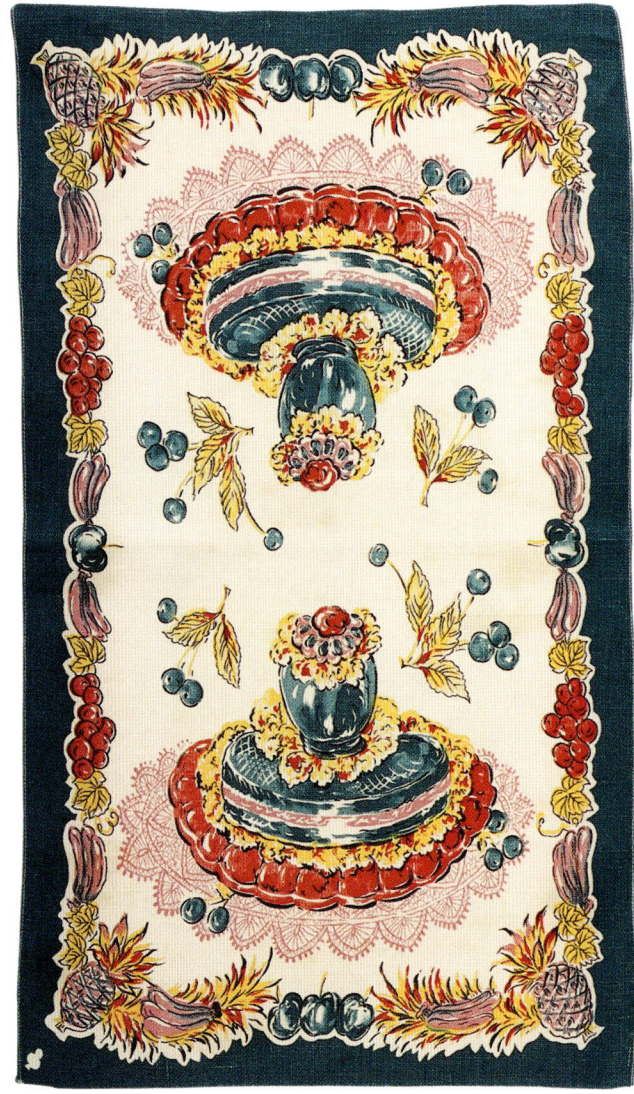

Confectionary towel showing a triple-layer dessert. The dessert sits on a pink lace doily and tiny fruit border all around. Price range: $15

Beverages

1960s design with alcoholic beverages lined up in their different shaped glasses. We see a martini, mug of beer, cognac, champagne, wine and more. Three bright red bar stools. Price range: $15

Scotch and Soda. Towel is decorated in a Scottish theme, and the woman and gentleman are both dressed in tartans. He holds a large bottle of scotch and she carries a spritzer bottle of soda. Price range $18

Happy hour towel showing names of different mixed drinks. Tipsy gentlemen holding bottles of liquor and hanging on to the lamp post and a lady sitting on a champagne glass. Note the "police riot squad" vehicle with the word "sidecar" below. Blue elephants border the towel. Price range: $18

69

Dancehall-girl sitting on the bar with a frothy beer in her hand. Her hourglass figure is encased in a red and white striped outfit edged in black lace. She wears a flamboyant hat and colorful bracelets. Sides are edged with beer mugs and various shaped bottles of liquor. Price range: $15

Festive scene, perhaps New Years Eve, is being celebrated here with ice bucket full of green ice cubes and a bottle of champagne. Corkscrew, ribbons and champagne glasses decorate the background. Note the hors d'oeuvre ball, which was popular in the 1950's to hold finger foods stylishly such as the olives shown here. Price range: $15

Vera towel done in beautiful lilac, orchid and soft blue. Wine bottles and the words "Schloss Belvedere." This has the Vera signature, but without the ladybug. Price range: $18

New Year's celebration. Champagne bottle and glass with confetti and ribbons on a red background. Price range: $15

Whiskey bottle with three dancing saloon girls on the label and the words "Bottled in Bond." Mixed drinks, a glass of wine and a soda water spritzer decorate the sides. Carrie Wilson signature in corner. Bottled in Bond refers to bourbon whiskey that meets the standards of the Bottled in Bond Act which passed in 1897. The Bottled in Bond Act stemmed from the desire of the Bourbon Whiskey industry to set dependable standards for whiskey distillers. In order to be called "bonded" whiskey, the whiskey had to meet certain requirements and among these were that it had to be legally-defined straight whiskey, distilled in a single season by a single distillery, and bottled at 100 proof. It also had to be stored in the bonded warehouse for four years before bottling. At this point the government would put its own green Bottled in Bond seal on every bottle. Artist: Carrie Wilson. Price range: $18

"On the house." Design shows a house with welcome mat along with bottles of wine, mugs of beer, limes, pretzels, and hors d'oeuvres. Price range: $18

Fun towel showing saloon girls and gents with glasses of mixed drinks. Sides show the titles of many different songs such as "Swanee River," "Old Black Joe," "Carry Me Back To Old Virginny," and more. Manufacturer: Leacock and Company. Price range: $15

Lady with red gloves and red shoes doing a happy somersault. Bottles of wine, bourbon and scotch and the words "what's yours?" Artist: Tom Morrow was an artist and illustrator, who created illustrations for the original productions of Broadway shows from the 1950s to the 1980s. His designs were seen in print ads, sheet music, textile goods, posters and show art from such Broadway shows as "Fiddler on the Roof," "Auntie Mame," "The Unsinkable Molly Brown," and others. He died in 1995. Manufacturer: Stevens Linen Associates. Price range: $18

"No Wolves Allowed." Here we have a dapper gentleman holding a martini in one hand with his other hand around a pretty girl's waist. Manufacturer: P & S Creations. Price range: $15

Cocktail shaker with martini glass and cherries. Price range: $15

Old-time western saloon design with cowboys, dancing girls, card games and bartender. The cowboys all have holsters with guns and wear cowboy boots and hats. The sides are lined with saddles, cards and pipes all painted in bright reds, yellows and greens. Price range: $22

Dancehall-girl and cabaret boy both dressed in their saloon finery, she with her fancy red skirt and feathered hat, he in his dancing shoes and bowler hat. Figures dance in the background and the sides are lined with old style lamps. Price range: $15

Anthropomorphic mixed drinks. Each drink wears an outfit to match their personality with the Daiquiri strumming a guitar and wearing a sombrero, the Uptown wears a tophat and the Scotch and Soda with a jaunty plaid cap. Price range: $18

This is a comical scene showing two tipsy little mice with one mouse tipping over a cocktail shaker while the other mouse holds up his martini glass to receive the golden elixir. Note how the artist has given them large oversized ears, long curly-cued tails and orange-lidded eyes. Artist signature don in corner. Prints Charming. Artist: don. Manufacturer: Sun Weave Linen Corporation, New York. Price range: $15

Red and white hobnail water jug design. Price range: $15

This pure linen towel, made in Ireland, highlights the recipe for Irish coffee along with Elsie the Cow smiling in the corner. Price range: $18

Matching apron. Price range: $18

This "Be Modern!" towel is a 1950s design with the pink wall oven and the philodendron plant in a stylish pink planter. The sides are decorated with mid-century designed beater, toaster and coffee pot. The star of the towel is the lady of the house – she is cooking while wearing a pretty dress, ruffled apron and fancy high-heeled shoes. Note the star burst clock on the wall. Predominate colors here are pastel pinks and greens. Price range: $20

A "Be Modern!" design. Sleek coffee pot, philodendrons, beater and starburst clock, all in 1950s pink, green and aqua blue. Price range: $20

Linen towel in orange and brown with coffee pot, plates and steaming cups of coffee. Price range: $15

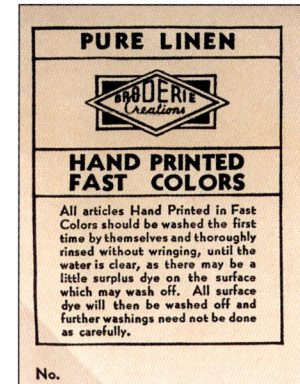

Broderie paper tag

Circa 1940s towel showing kitchen items in pink and blue. Old-style toaster and refrigerator, double glass coffee pot, and cups and saucers. Price range: $15

Such a cheerful towel all in blues and yellows. Large coffee pot with mixing bowl and spoon, sugar shaker and cup and saucer. Price range: $15

Coffee pot, cup, saucer, and creamer decorate the ends with a diamond design throughout. Towel retains the manufacturer's "Broderie Creations" sticker. Manufacturer: A. R. Rosenthal & Co. Inc. Price range: $15

Linen towel in red and white. Steaming tea pot with the words "tea towel" formed from the steam. Price range: $15

Pottery, dancing figures and Cameos in white, soft green and gold. This is a Paragon Needlecraft towel titled "Dance of the Hours" inspired by Wedgwood. Beautiful classical pure linen towel. Manufacturer: Paragon Needlecraft. Price range: $18

This is a fabulous design showing a Chinese gentleman with a steaming bowl of egg-drop soup. Pictures of rice cakes and tea, Chow Mein, and rice. Food items such as onions, lobsters, mushroom, duck, and fish decorate the sides. The background is pink and all the items are accented with metallic gold. Manufacturer: Town and Country Linen Corporation, importers and manufacturers of table linens, kitchen textiles, pillows, throws, and bath products. David and Jeffrey Beyda run this family-owned textile company, which was started in 1953 when their grandfather sold handkerchiefs from a pushcart in the streets of Manhattan. Price range: $20

Town & Country Linen Corporation horse and carriage mark.

"Let's read the tea-leaves!" Towel is covered with small squares, each one with a symbol and the prophecy it foretells. An instruction on how to read tea leaves is given with notes such as "the symbols shown at the top of cup predict the events of the near future." "Martha" signature in corner of towel. Price range: $15

Brightly colored paint palette design. Price range: 18

Calories

Humorous calorie towel depicting a large woman standing on a scale and the arrow hitting 500 pounds. Lists different food items with the calorie amounts and shows food and drink items with warning next to them. A martini and mug of beer, "you'll get a 'hangover' in more places than one!" A cube of butter, "you 'butter' not!" A fun and colorful towel. Price range: $15

This is a linen towel put out by Sweet'N Low sugar substitute. Shows a lady sitting on a scale and she has been an angel about watching her calories. Many items are listed with calorie amounts, and a sugar equivalent chart for packets of Sweet'N Low compared to sugar is shown. Price range: $15

Calorie towel showing a frustrated lady on a scale. "It's the little things that count." Price range: $15

Lady on a scale and colorful pictures of food with their calorie amounts all around. Notice how the owner of this cloth appliquéd a dress onto the woman. Price range: $15

Pure linen calories towel showing everything from "chocolate bar" at 350 calories to "caviar" at 50 calories. Even a box full of chocolate candy with no calorie count, simply the word "danger." Manufacturer: Hedaya Bros. Price range: $15

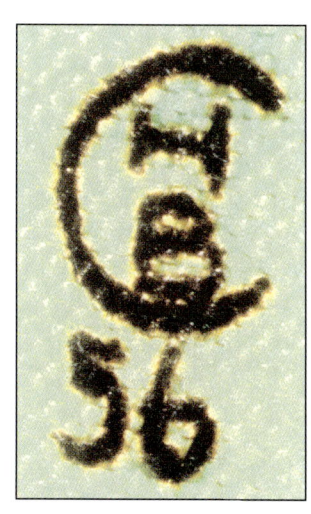

Hedaya Brothers linens would often show their "HB" logo in a corner of the item along with the design date, as shown here.

Calorie towel paper tag. Dated "1952 Hedaya Bros."

The healthy fruit, vegetables and fish decorate the sides with the desirable higher calorie fondue and wine in the corners. Startex. Manufacturer: Spartan Mills. Price range: $15

Calorie Weeping Towel. Two ladies, one with a slender figure, the other one amply proportioned. Gives the calorie count of miscellaneous foods and drinks. Next time you feel the urge for a cocktail you may want to go for a drink of gin as it has only 75 calories while an Old Fashioned has a whopping 200. Next to the larger lady, it reads "Well we can't all be scrawny." Price range: $15

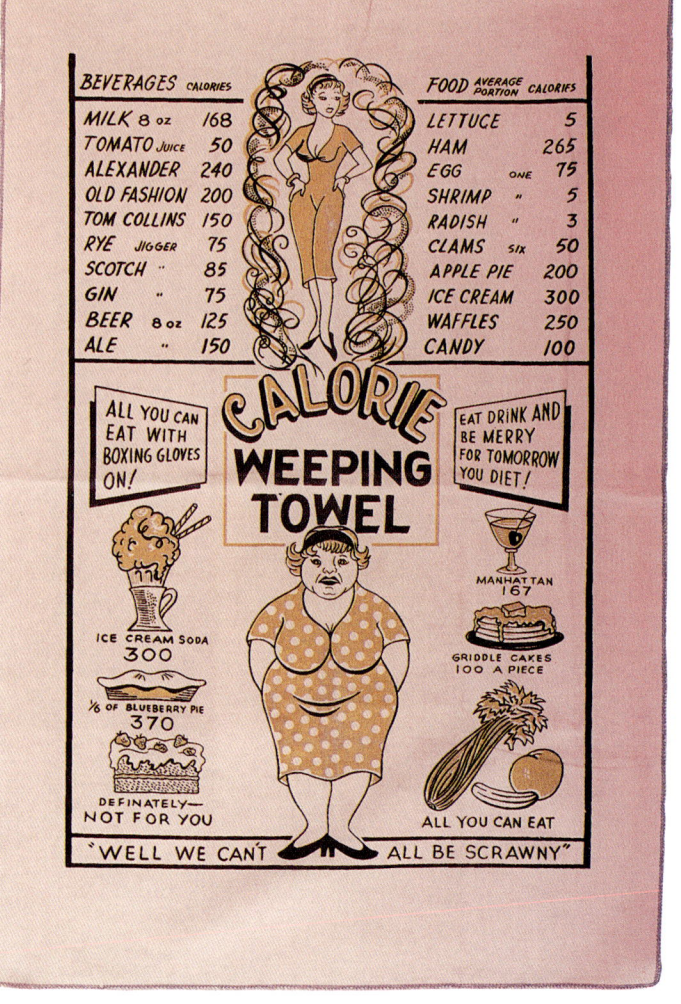

Outdoors

Farms

Bucilla foil tag

Farmer and wife in the garden with the farmer pushing a wheelbarrow full of colorful vegetables and the wife totes an overflowing fruit basket. Price range: $15

Farm boy harvesting apples. Cute scene of boy wearing red overalls and sporting blue and white polka dotted scarf and handkerchief. Baskets of apples at his feet and the sides are bordered with fruit. Price range: $15

Farm scene with boy and girl. They both carry pails and are at the water well. Farm implements such as plow, rake, shovel and clippers line the sides. Manufacturer: Artmark. Price range: $15

This towel advertises Texaco products and shows a red Texaco gas truck winding through the farmland. "It pays to farm with Texaco Products." The gas truck is a 1934 Diamond T Doodlebug tanker. Startex. Manufacturer: Spartan Mills. Price range: $25

Young man and woman happily dancing with barn and silo in the background. Well pumps, chicken on her nest, and bags of grain decorate the border. Trees and flowers with smiling faces line the sides. Price range: $15

Farmer chasing chickens. Colorful barn in the background, stalks of corn and red wood fence. Manufacturer: Bucilla. Price range: $18

Artmark tag

Same background scene as Farmer towel, this one showing his wife holding a rooster. Manufacturer: Bucilla. Price range: $15

Montgomery Ward 1956 catalog page showing the farmer towels with matching tablecloth, apron and accessories. "Quaint country boy and girl play leading roles in the colorful rural scenes pictured in this unique kitchen set." Towels originally priced at 89 cents each.

Barn scene with silo and weather vane. This is a detailed sectional design of a barn showing the interior rooms with a cow and many different types of farm implements. This towel was designed along with a similar towel which had a sectional design showing the interior of a farm house. Linen. Artist: Luther Travis. Manufacturer: Town and Country Linens. Price range: $15

What a cute design with little boy holding a hoe and surrounded by poultry, a baby lamb and a rabbit. Note the checked design of the boy's pants and the white picket fence bordering the towel edge. Price range: $15

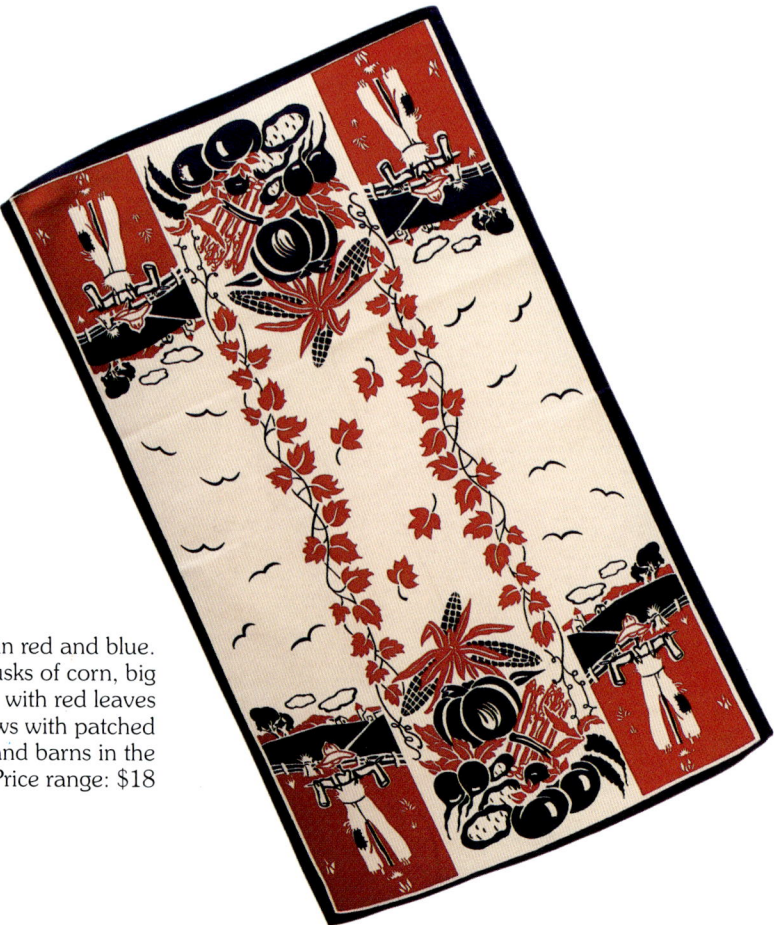

Vegetable harvest towel in red and blue. Bunches of asparagus, husks of corn, big blue pumpkin and more with red leaves down the center. Scarecrows with patched overalls, floppy hats, silos, and barns in the background. Price range: $18

Noah's Ark design with a boat full of animals. Elephants, donkeys, tigers, penguins and more decorate this cloth in red and burgundy. Note the rainbow in the background and the swirling ocean scene with fish, shark and sea horses. Price range: $15

Garden design with a pair of garden gloves with rakes, shovel and hoe, and the sides are decorated with packets of vegetable seeds. Artist: Tammis Keefe. Margaret Thomas Keefe is most well known for her handkerchief designs. She also designed scarves and household linens including tablecloths and towels. Price range: $18

Dutch boy holding his newly carved wooden boat with a happy look on his face. Sailboat bobbing in the water, windmill in the background and a border of tulips and wooden clogs all around. Price range: $15

Art Deco design with gazelles and bellflowers. This is a printed Vogart towel with the Vogart name shown in corner of towel. Price range: $15

Sailor boy looking through telescope. Comical faces in portholes around the border. Price range: $22

Milkman in his delivery carriage with green and white horse. Artist: Tom Lamb. 1896-1988. Thomas Babbitt Lamb was an artist, inventor and children's books author. He is most famous for his children's handkerchief designs, which are very popular today. He also designed household linens such as towels, tablecloths, and napkins. His signed towels are sought after by collectors for their often colorful and fun designs. Price range: $28

Oriental design with geisha girl in carriage and a pagoda in background. Decorative items such as fans and vases line the border. Price range: $15

Red haired lady wearing riding breeches stands next to a fireplace enjoying a plate of food and a drink. Reads "C'est pour rire" and "Sore tail." Copyright 1950 by Fred Pearson, 2nd and Richard Taylor. Towel retains the original store price tag from "G. Fox & Co. Hartford." Price was $1.00. Price range: $18

Modes of transportation. Horse and buggy, air balloon, Model A Ford, and a World War II airplane. Retains "Victory K&B" sticker. Manufacturer: Kemp & Beatley Inc., New York, founded in 1919. Kitchen linens are still produced under the Kemp & Beatley name, now a division of Ex-Cell Home Fashions. Price range: $18

Victory K&B tag.

Christmas

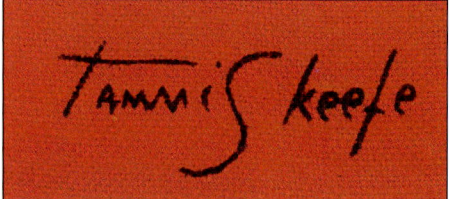

Tammis Keefe signature

Robert Darr Wert paper tag

Shiny Christmas tree ornaments in many designs including birds, bells and strawberries. Manufacturer: Stevens. Price range: $15

Deck the halls with boughs of holly. Holly wreath and angels. Artist: Tammis Keefe. Manufacturer: Fallani & Cohn. Price range: $18

Robert Darr Wert Christmas design. Price range: $15

Snow covered street lamps decorated with holly and pine with the North Star shining in the background. Note the Town and Country Linen horse and carriage mark in the corner. Manufacturer: Town and Country Linen. Price range: $13

Christmas design with reindeer, ornaments and singers. Angels with a trumpet and harp, a tree lit with candles and little angels on clouds, all done in pastel pinks and blues with gold metallic highlights. Price range: $18

This is a very detailed towel showing angels with trumpets, ornaments on ribbons and a village with church steeple. Bells, shooting stars, elves and tiny angels with wands, all done in red, green and metallic gold. Price range: $18

Christmas design with elves carrying peppermint canes, reindeer wearing big red bows, and tiny angels singing. Christmas colors of red, green and metallic gold. Price range: $18

This 29 wide x 53 long piece of cloth was cut from bolt cloth. There are three towels here with each design measuring 15 ½ x 27 inches. Cutting lines are between each towel to guide a straight cut and there is additional fabric in length and width to allow for hemming. Parisian Prints. Manufacturer: Joseph Sultan and Sons. Price range: $20

Florals

Large red hibiscus flowers with green leaves and a scalloped red border. This is toweling fabric which was cut from the bolt to make towels, runners, napkins, or curtains. This piece measures 17 inches wide by 19 feet long. Fabric pieces such as this are desirable due to the very long length, unused condition and beautiful floral pattern. Price range: $60

Display of flowers and fruit including blue carnations, plump pink roses, cherries and grapes. The sides are bordered with a blue ribbon tied into a bow at each end, and entwined within it are tiny clusters of fruit and flowers. Note the accent of white given to the fruits for a shiny appearance. A Technicolor Print. Manufacturer: Eaton. Price range: $15

This 34 wide x 37 long piece of cloth was cut from bolt cloth. There are two runners, each with a beautiful floral design measuring 15 ½ x 35 inches. Cutting lines are between each towel to guide a straight cut, and there is additional fabric in length and width to allow for hemming. Price range: $20

Red wire basket filled with red, yellow and green flowers. Flowers edge the towel all around and a green bow decorates the basket. Price range: $15

Bouquets of pansies and sweet pea blossoms. Price range: $15

Large pink with burgundy roses and rosebuds on a red grid background. Cut from the bolt and unused, this linen fabric measures 17 x 81 inches. Price range: $22

Magnificent large pink roses with shades of red and burgundy. Scalloped red border with rosebuds scattered about. This towel was sold in the Sears, Roebuck and Company 1950 Spring and Summer catalog. Startex. Manufacturer: Spartan Mills. Price range: $18

Page from the 1950 Sears, Roebuck and Company Spring and Summer catalog showing the Startex rose towel. Described as "35% linen, 65% cotton for extra absorbency and economy. Vivid color print." Priced at three for $1.14.

Blue dahlias, red flowers and yellow tinged green leaves with blue bleeding hearts trailing from bouquet. Price range: $15

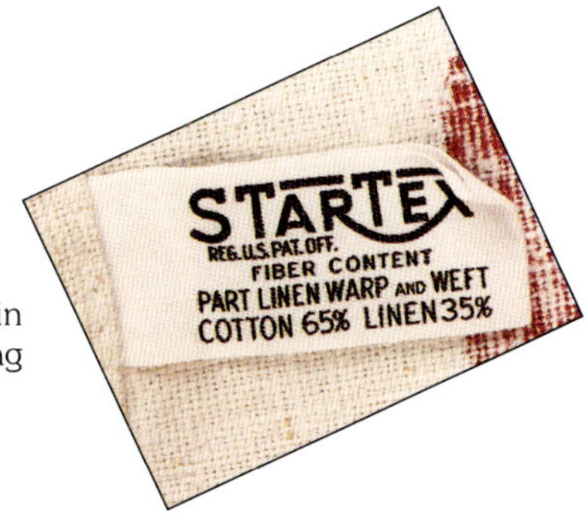

Startex sewn-in tag

Same design with green border and pink bow. Hadson. Manufacturer: Carolina Mfg. Price range: $15

Straw baskets full of mixed flowers. Both baskets decorated with blue bows. Hadson. Manufacturer: Carolina Mfg. Price range: $15

Clover plant with red flowers and green shamrocks. Two gray pigs decorate one end. Startex. Manufacturer: Spartan Mills. Price range: $15

Large orange poppies with leaves and blue bow. Towel retains price tag and original sticker which reads "A Technicolor Print." Priced at 50 cents. Manufacturer: Eaton. Price range: $15

Bouquet of tulips and mixed posies tied with a blue bow. Floral border all around. This manufacturer, Eaton, would often print the Eaton name in tiny letters hidden within the towel design. The colors on Novelty brand print towels are brilliant and beautiful when new, but fade quickly when laundered. Because of their tendency to fade, these towels are best used for display only. If necessary, wash quickly by hand in lukewarm water with no soaking. Novelty. Manufacturer: Eaton. Price range: $18.

Notice the small Startex star in the corner.

Eaton name.

97

Oversized red poppies with white daisies, blue cornflowers and nodding yellow bells. The bright poppies have a dark shading to add a rich depth to the colors. Manufacturer: Weil & Durrsé. Price range: $20

Weil & Durrsé tag

White dogwoods on a blue background. Manufacturer: California Hand Prints, Hermosa Beach, California. California Handprints manufactured plain and printed textile piece goods made of cotton, synthetic fibers or mixtures thereof. Began their business in 1936. Known for their kitchen textiles fabricated from all cotton, a rayon/cotton blend, and a nylon/cotton blend which were named after southern California towns including Hermosa, Coronado, Del Mar, Pasadena and Laguna. They produced linens under the brand names California Hand Prints, Screen Master Prints, California Imports International, Cuprashan, California Authentics, Tic-Toc, Thompson of California, and Silkstone. One can find the popular California Hand Prints linens with several different types of tags including California Hand Prints, Thompson California Hand Prints, and Thompson Hand Prints. Price range: $15

This Startex fabric is still on the bolt, measuring 16 inches wide and 37 feet long. Fabricated from a blend of 75% cotton and 25% linen, it has a beautiful design of red chrysanthemums alternating with swirls of blue. The bolt end retains the Startex Twinkle "Printowling" paper label. Startex. Manufacturer: Spartan Mills. $90.

Mixed floral bouquet with forget me nots, tulips and more, with border of flowers. Towel retains G W Prismacolor sticker and original store price tag from Sears, Roebuck and Co. Price was 39 cents. OPA price. Manufacturer: Grossman & Weissman. Price range: $18

Blue lattice basket filled with pink, yellow and blue flowers. Manufacturer: Fruit of the Loom. Price range: $15

Off the bolt floral toweling measuring 18 inches wide by 6 feet long. Flower clusters with red edged floral border. Shown sold in Sears catalog. Price range: $30

Blue and red chrysanthemums and berries with a red border. Shown sold in Sears catalog. Price range: $15

Sears, Roebuck 1945 catalog. "Make it yourself from colorful printed scarfing." The flower cluster toweling is shown as (C) and described "Durable cotton twill. A lovely scarfing that will give long service. Brighten up your kitchen or dinette with matching sets. State choice of red or blue. 18 inches wide. Yard 49 cents." The chrysanthemum toweling is shown as (A) and described "Printed rayon and linen. There's no limit to the number of matching pieces you can make out of this floral pattern scarfing. Draperies, towels, scarfs can all match. About 17 inches wide. Yard 39 cents."

One side of this towel shows a Dutch boy with a wheelbarrow full of tulips and red windmill behind him. The other side shows a girl in a long dress and apron carrying a bouquet of flowers. Note the green hat the girl wears and the patched seat and knees of the boys pants. Manufacturer: Artmark. Price range: $15

Tropical scene with sailboats on the ocean, palm trees and Polynesian ladies wearing floral leis. Hadson. Manufacturer: Carolina Mfg. Price range: $15

Picket gate with a watering can and a clay pot full of tulips. Small flower pots and watering cans dot the background and floral border all around, done in blue and gold. Price range: $15

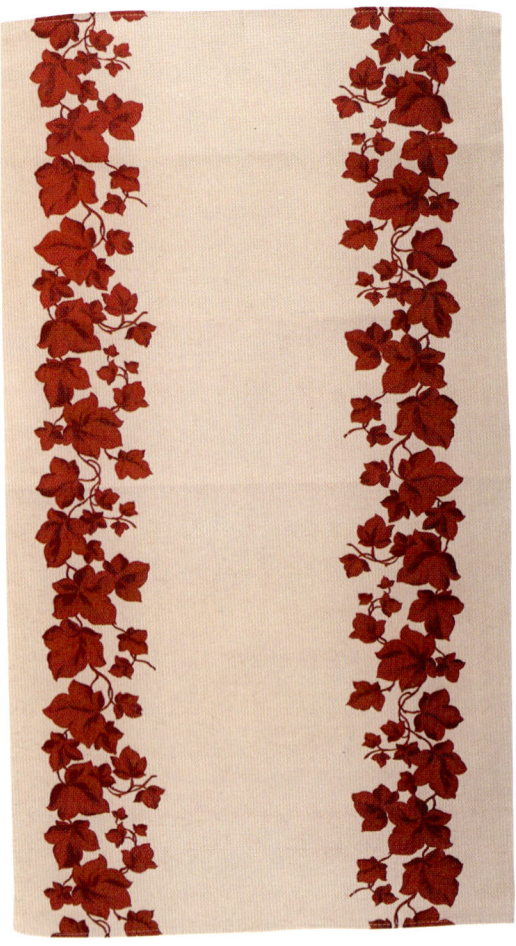

Startex ivy design in red. Shown in the accompanying catalog page and described as: "Charming vine print for kitchen harmony. Make breakfast sets, table runners and chair covers as well as window curtains and dish towels." Priced at 5 yards $1.40. Price range: $12

Page from Sears Roebuck and Co. 1945 catalog *Colorful Kitchen Toweling and Towels*.

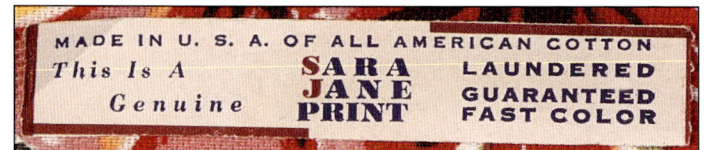

Sara Jane tag

Morning Glory. Morning glories on a blue background. Tag states "Genuine Sara Jane Print." Shown in the accompanying catalog page and described as "Morning Glory unusual in color, design. Rosy morning-glories cluster on scalloped border and bold center stripes of dark blue. Size 17 x 24 in." Priced at two for 75 cents. Price range: $18

Beautiful floral designs, as shown in the Sears catalog page shown on page 102.

Large floral display in green and blue vase. Blue daisies and blue bows with black polka dots trim the sides. Retains the original "Hadson" sticker. Hadson. Manufacturer: Carolina Mfg. Price range: $15

Birds

Art Deco era towel in tan and brown colors on linen. The birds are cross with the whistling tea pot. Price range: $15

Fat red and black birds chirping a song. Musical notes fill the center and the sides are edged with flowers. Price range: $15

Cotton towel in red and white showing unique design of road runners running and observing the flowers on a ribbon trail. Artist: Harwood Steiger. Price range: $15

Bird's nest.

Nest of bright yellow baby birds ready to be fed. Colorful adult birds on a cherry blossom branch. Print by Technicolor. Manufacturer: Eaton. Price range: $15

This towel shows black and red birds flying about each with a different recipe in their beaks. Each recipe is for a day of the week, for instance, Thursday is "Doughnuts" and the recipe is 1 cup sugar, 4 cups flour, 1 tspn soda, 1 cup sour cream, grated nutmeg and 3 eggs. Price range: $15

1930s singing bird design on linen.

Birds and Bees. Two chirping birds on a branch with striped gold and black bees flitting about clover blossoms. Beehive in each corner. Price range: $15

Branches of berries and fruit blossoms with mama and baby birds. Beautiful bluebird with wings spread. Print by Technicolor. Although the Technicolor towels are quite bright when new, the colors fade quickly when laundered. Launder any Technicolor print in lukewarm water with the least amount of soaking necessary, and use only for display, if you wish to retain the rich colors. Manufacturer: Eaton. Price range: $15

Design showing an eagle with a banner "Don't Give Up The Ship" along with stars and stripes. "Don't Give Up The Ship" is a favorite motto of the United States Navy. These were the dying words of Commander James Lawrence during a battle in the War of 1812. Artist Name: Mary Sarg (1911-1986). Price range: $22

Mary Sarg Murphy was a painter, illustrator and decorative artist, and an accomplished portrait painter. She was strongly influenced by her father, Tony Sarg, a decorative artist, illustrator and puppeteer. Murphy began her art career decorating boxes and furniture for the Tony Sarg Shops in New Hope and in Nantucket, where the Sarg family spent their summers from 1923 on. She later designed fabrics, wallpapers, children's clothing and towels for the shops. In the 1930's, she was well-known for her illustrations in such magazines at Today, Woman's Day, and Mademoiselle, as well as illustrating children's books.

Cats and Dogs

A pet lover's favorite towel. Happy dog with black spots and big pink eyes, surrounded by puppies. Other end shows a smiling cat with gray stripes and a kitten in her arms, with white kittens around her. The background is pink and the cats and dogs are all done in pink, gray, and black. Artist: C. P. Meier. Price range: $15

Linen towel in a 1960's design with sleek cats covered with a red rose design. Fancy red tassels decorate the sides. Artist: Virginia Zito, whose signature is in the corner. Price range: $15

Large cat face on a simple red and white background. Price range: $15

Hardy Craft tag.

Leacock paper sticker and "Martha" signature.

Brown faced kittens with black stripes nestled among yellow pussy willows decorate both ends of this towel. They wear big bows that match the color of the butterflies along the sides. Note the beautiful black and lime green eyes of the kittens. Artist: Martha. Manufacturer: Leacock and Company. Price range: $15

Siamese cat in black, white and gray with a little gray mouse scurrying away. Price range: $15

Sleek cats and kitten sitting on orange with polka dots pillows. The gold cat wears a big orange and black bow and a ball of yarn rolls along the towel sides. Hardy Craft. Manufacturer: James G. Hardy & Co, Inc., New York. Founded by James G. Hardy in 1929. Produced tablecloths, napkins, runners, crash piece goods, and all manner of household linens. This company remains in the textile business today, producing kitchen linens. Although it is no longer owned by the James Hardy family, it retains the name James Hardy & Company. Price range: $15

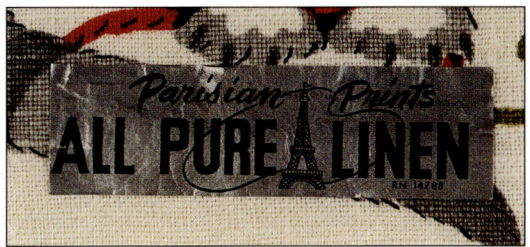

Parisian Prints tag.

Cat with gray stripes and wearing a big orange bow is surrounded by her favorite things such as a ball of yarn, bowl of milk and fish and mouse toys. Manufacturer: Joseph Sultan and Sons (JS&S). This textiles company produces tablecloths, towels, place mats, bath mats, household textiles, and Christmas, Halloween, and Hanukah products. They produced many vintage kitchen linens, including tablecloths and towels under the brand names Parisian Prints, Exclusive, JS&S, and Sultan Creations. Founded in 1928 by Joseph Sultan, Joseph Sultan and Sons continues to be a thriving business run by fourth generation Sultan family member Joseph Sultan, the founder's namesake and great grandson. They now use the name "Sultan Linens." Price range: $15

It's a Dogs' Life! This appears to be a day in the life of your typical doggie housewife. She is wearing an apron and diligently drying the dishes. Along the sides are vignettes of her vacuuming, ironing a pair of pants, and cooking. Price range: $15

Another design in the "It's a Dogs' Life!" series. This gray Scottie dog sits on a pink stool and stirs a bowl of something good. Little pictures along the sides show her with a purse on her arm off on a shopping spree, hanging clothes on the line, and patching a pair of pants. The colors are 50's pink and aqua green. Price range: $15

Big eyed white puppy with branches of white dogwood blossoms. Butterflies flit about and pink blossoms line the sides. Artist: Martha. Manufacturer: Leacock and Company. Price range: $15

Bull dog with red collar. Border of dog bowls, milk bones, cans of Pard, Kennel Ration, and Gaines. Price range: $18

Gray poodle wearing an apron and flipping pancakes. She wears a chefs hat, a studded collar and yellow ribbons on her ears. Big green eyes. The sides are lined with eggs, egg beaters, champagne bottle and champagne glass. Parisian Prints. Price range: $15

Charming design of fluffy gray poodle wheeling her little poodle puppy in a fancy green baby carriage. Note the gay green ribbon tied around mama poodle's neck and the puppy holding a green lollipop. Carriage and towel border edged with green rayon ruffle. Imperial Creations. Price range: $15

Scottish Terriers

Many towels have designs that include a Scottish Terrier, or Scottie. The Scottie dogs' popularity began when this breed of dog was recognized by the American Kennel Club in the late 1800s. By the 1920s, the breed became popular as pets and their image was placed on toys, planters, figurines, clothing, and more. During U. S. President Franklin Delano Roosevelt's term, from 1933 to 1945, the Scottish Terrier's popularity soared. The president owned a Scottish Terrier named Fala. Pictures of the president with little Fala became commonplace during the first few years of World War II and soon his image was used on merchandise, including ashtrays, fabric, tablecloths, towels, cigarette boxes, whiskey bottles, and pictures.

Housemaid and two Scottie dogs, one black, one white. The dogs have their paws up on the table anxious for that plate of cookies and she shoos them away. One side of towel shows wine glass, jugs, gravy servers and more all in stripes and polka dots. Hadson. Manufacturer: Carolina Mfg. Price range: $18

People

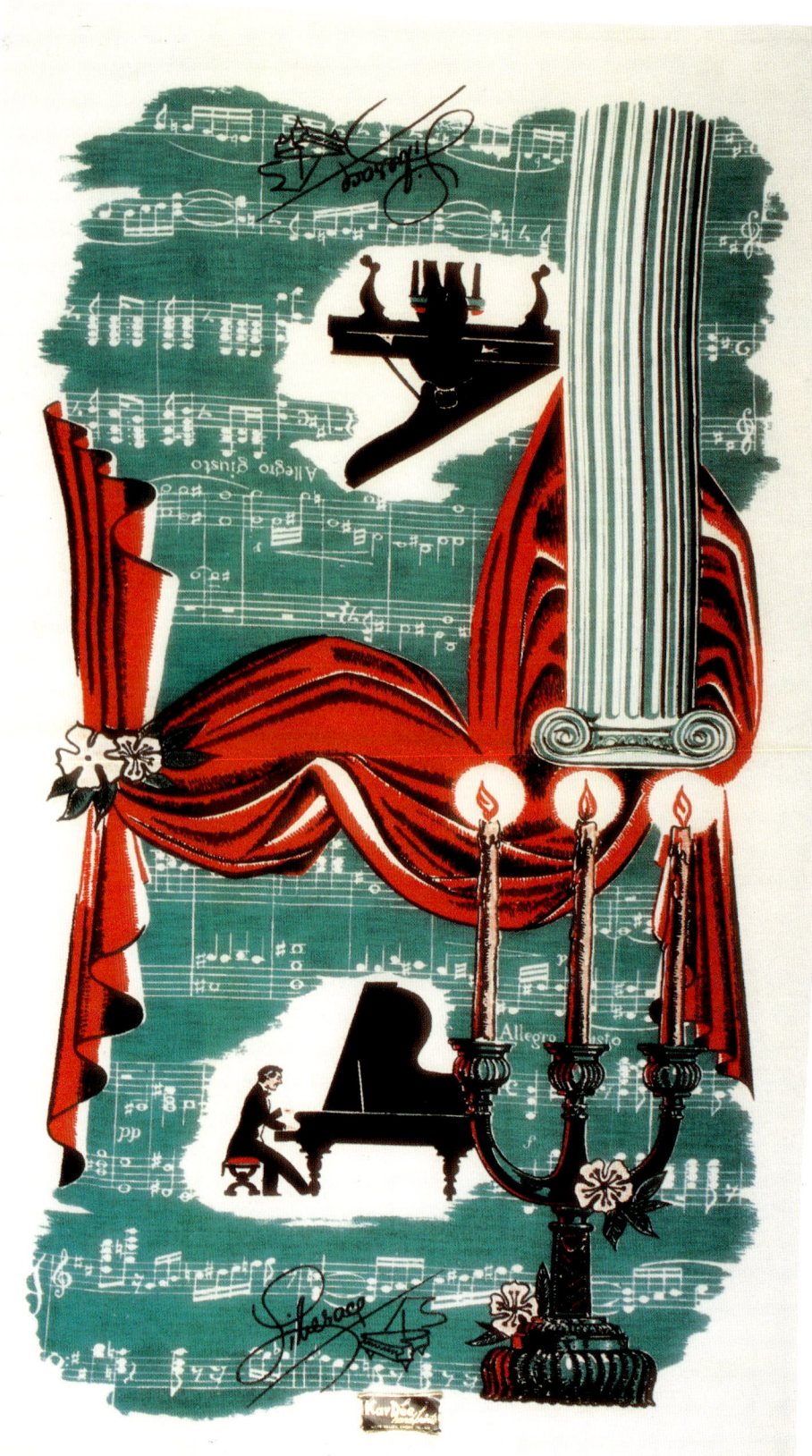

This design shows the entertainer Liberace, Wladziu Valentino Liberace (1919-1987), playing the piano, with his signature and a sketch of his piano at each end of the towel. Elegant background with red curtains, musical notes, and Liberace's trademark candelabra with electric lights. Liberace was a flamboyant American pianist and showman, often called "Mr. Showmanship" for his magnificent costumes, joyful music, and dazzling charisma. Manufacturer: Kay Dee Handprints. Price range: $25

KayDee Handprints, Inc. was founded in 1951 by Jacques Delaporte in Hope Valley, Rhode Island. The company sold towels, pot holders, wall hangings, women's tote bags, and kitchen calendars, all hand-screened on linen fabric. Many well known textile artists designed for KayDee Handprints, including Sewell Jackson, Lois Long, Robert Hughes, John L. Gieroch, Edward C. Smith, Bob Goryl, Richard Batchelder, Victor Beals, and Robert Darr Wert.
KayDee Handprints towels are popular with linen collectors today and one can find their vintage towels in many designs still with the KayDee stickers attached. They produced towels in many different designs, including themes such as Americana, bridges, calendars, light houses, and tourist souvenir towels. Although no longer owned by the Delaporte family, the company operates currently as Kay Dee Designs. It continues to produce kitchen linens, incorporating many of their vintage designs along with popular modern designs, and has partnered with well-known textile designers, such as Sue Zipkin, Lisa Audit, Theresa Kasun, Deb Strain, and others. Kay Dee Designs remains a thriving textile manufacturer under the leadership of current owners Chuck Donnell and Rick Rakauskas.

Garden Girls

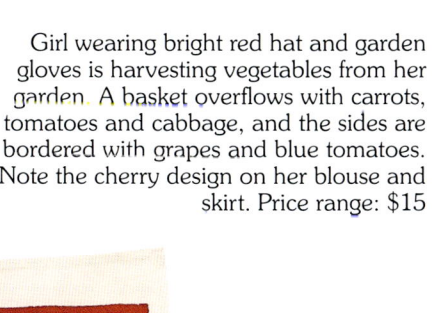

Girl wearing bright red hat and garden gloves is harvesting vegetables from her garden. A basket overflows with carrots, tomatoes and cabbage, and the sides are bordered with grapes and blue tomatoes. Note the cherry design on her blouse and skirt. Price range: $15

Harvesting beets from the garden. Towel bordered all around with red picket fence edged with vegetables. Note the red overalls of the girl and her yellow straw hat. Price range: $15

Garden girl gathering fresh tomatoes surrounded by berries, zucchini, bell peppers and radishes. Spading fork and shovel cross in center. Price range: $15

Garden girl weeding her garden of corn and cabbages. Red bow in her hair, and a red picket fence encloses the garden. Side display of green beans, strawberries, carrots and more. Price range: $15

Windmill in the background with a young girl riding her bike through a field of tulips. Price range: $15

Garden girl preparing a harvest of vegetables for canning. Abundant fruits and vegetables border the cloth with red apples, yellow carrots, red grapes and large red fork and spoon in center. Price range: $15

Preparing to milk the cow. Border of vegetables, clover, fruit and wheat. Note her blue outfit with matching blue hair bow and her little yellow milking stool. Price range: $15

Girl cutting oversized blue cherries off the vine. She wears a blue scarf, hoop skirt and red flared blouse. Blue cherries and bellflowers line the ends. Note the scissors she uses to harvest the cherries. The owner of this towel added a colorful trim of hand done tatting to each end. Broderie Creations. Manufacturer: A. R. Rosenthal & Co. Inc. Price range: $22

Dutch girl towel painted in soft pastels. She carries a basket of pink and yellow flowers, the sides are decorated with tulips and daffodils and there is a pink windmill in the background. Price range: $15

Lovely orchardist gathering fruit, in this case red lemons. She is holding a bowl to capture the freshly squeezed green lemon juice. Broderie Creations. Manufacturer: A. R. Rosenthal & Co. Inc. Price range: $22

Cart full of red tulips and birds flying about carrying tulips in their beaks. Broderie Creations. Manufacturer: A. R. Rosenthal & Co. Inc. Price range: $22

Garden girl with armload of tulips. Note the unusual beauty of this girl and the many bright colors here. Over sized blue bow on her wide skirt and she wears a green hat with a red bow. Tulips and hyacinth line the sides. Hadson. Manufacturer: Carolina Mfg. Price range: $18

Girl off to market with a basket full of produce on her arm. The flowers and fruit have a gingham design and she wears a blue and black polka dot ribbon in her hair. Note her sweet red high-heeled shoes and the green ruffle on her skirt. Price range: $15

Southern belle in billowing skirt and carrying a parasol stands next to a sundial. She wears black lacy gloves and a red hat with a feather. Price range: $18

Garden girl with a wheelbarrow full of vegetables fresh from her garden. Price range: $15

Girl in orchard gathering apples and two apple trees loaded with yellow and red fruit. She wears a red hat with flowers and a long yellow apron, which she uses to hold the harvested fruit. Along the sides are cottages surrounded by white-capped mountains, and clusters of pears, apples and grapes. Price range: $15

Young woman standing next to roses and hollyhocks, and she carries a basket of fresh picked flowers. Her red hat is lined with yellow daisies. Note the many layers of her dress with over-skirts of red with bows, a swoop of gold and the top skirt edged in lace. Price range: $15

Girl carrying basket of vegetables with vegetables lining the towel edge. Note her dainty blue sandals, red earrings and her gaily-colored skirt decorated with big red hibiscus flowers. Price range: $15

Imperial gold foil tag

Black-haired lady on floral covered swing. Her beautiful lace edged skirt is the border of the towel. The body of the towel made of linen and the ruffle made of rayon. Imperial Creations. Price range: $15

Imperial Linens mixer cover.
Price range: $15

120

Imperial Linens apron.
Price range: $15

Happy girl wearing a red frock and green striped apron, and holding a big yellow carrot. She must be off to the fair to enter her prized carrot in the largest vegetable division – certainly, she will win the blue ribbon. Price range: $18

Smiling farm girl holding a rooster and surrounded by poultry. Her brightly colored red and white polka dot dress has a white rayon ruffle. Note the saucy pantaloons and fancy black shoes she is wearing. Imperial Creations. Price range: $15

Imperial Linens toaster cover. Price range: $15

Beautiful pastels.

Dancers

Senorita with colorful flowery skirt dances with her partner. Tropical background with cactus, palm trees, mountains and white capped sea. Price range: $15

Beautiful girl dances while the gentleman plays his guitar. Tea pots, fruit bowls full of fruit, candelabras and flowers line the sides. Yellow palm trees with blue coconuts. Note the blue bows on her shoes and the red touch to the many ruffles on her skirt. Price range: $15

Beautiful senorita with a yellow flowery hat and high heeled red shoes. Her gay skirt is covered with a hibiscus flower design and trimmed in multi colored flounce. Price range: $15

Dancing girl wearing a serape and colorful skirt. The owner of this beautiful towel added hand crocheted trim to match the colors of the design. Price range: $15

Spanish dancers with musicians and palm trees in the background. Their dancing clothes are beautiful and elaborate and the lady wears necklace, bracelets and big earrings. Price range: $15

Two towels in a boxed gift set with bow. Each towel measures 14 x19 inches and shows a dancing couple. Set retains the JS&S Exclusive gold foil label. Manufacturer: Joseph Sultan and Sons (JS&S). Price range: $21

Hadson towel paper tags.

This figure is exceptionally beautiful due to its fine detailing such as the red flowing ribbon on her hat to the buttons on the back of her blouse. Factory machine stitched form and details with panties, skirt and scalloped plaid ruffle fabric. She seems bashful as she has turned her head away. Why? Manufacturer: Imperial Linens. Price range: $18

Oh! Now we understand….

Indian chief with child and woman dancing around the fire. Musical notes border the cloth. Hadson. Manufacturer: Carolina Mfg. Price range: $15

Beautiful linen towel showing porcelain figurines of Victorian lady and gentleman. Soft pastel colors of pink, green and blue with gold scrolling down the sides. Manufacturer: Garden State Prints, New York. Price range: $15

Beautiful Spanish woman holding a red rose and carrying a fan. Baskets of roses and smiling apples decorate the border. Note her colorful and flamboyant dress with floral fringed scarf. Broderie Creations. Manufacturer: A. R. Rosenthal & Co. Inc. Price range: $22

Gentleman in his Scottish tartan kilts being served a meal by the lady of the house. Blazing fire in the hearth, cuckoo clock, flowers, and a Scottie dog at his masters side. The other end shows gentleman in kilts playing bagpipes with little girl and boy in traditional costumes dancing to the music. Castle in the background and tulips border all around. Towel retains the "Hadson" sticker. Hadson. Manufacturer: Carolina Mfg. Price range: $15

Happy dancing couple holding glasses of champagne. Decorated with bottles of liquor, a spilled glass of wine, balloons and a smoking cigarette. Price range: $18

Everyone is smiling here with a bottle of wine on the table and two gentlemen enjoying their drinks. Lady wearing sexy skirt and tiny top entertaining them. Flowers, lobster, champagne glass with cherry, and an anthropomorphic sausage to top off this unusual towel. Hadson. Manufacturer: Carolina Mfg. Price range: $18

Can-Can cutie. Blonde haired lady with voluptuous figure doing the can-can. She wears a colorful frilly skirt and shows her red garters. The sides are decorated with ribbons, fans and small figures of dancing girls. Price range: $15

Servants

Cigar smoking chef carries a pretty maid around on his wagon. She is sitting on a stack of dinner plates and holds a tray with turkey on it. Price range: $18

Delightful scene showing a chef flipping pancakes and a maid catching them on a plate mid-air. The chef has the typical "Chef" black moustache and he wears white gloves while he cooks. Price range: $18

Pretty housemaid puts smiles on the faces of the milk and ice deliverymen. Artist: Zito. Towel retains the tag "JBM Original Creation." Price range: $18

Black butler holding a tray with a bottle of liquor and two glasses. Along his side is a dog with a big red bow around his neck and he carries a bucket of ice with a bottle of champagne. Ice tongs, glasses with cherries and wine, and ice buckets with bottles of spirits decorate the sides. Price range: $28

Comical scene with a waitress startled by a mouse. Note the wily look on the mouse's face. Price range: $15

This towel shows a different picture on each end. One is a black mammy with a steaming pot of stew and the other shows a butler carrying a beverage on a tray with a towel folded over his arm. Price range: $28

Pretty maid holding a tray with a spilled glass. Manufacturer: Bucilla. Price range: $18

Butler and maid dressed in purple and green with the border decorated with wine glasses. The maid is spilling her tray of drinks while a puppy pulls the rug out from under her feet. Price range: $18

Household staff with chef, maid, and butler, "Morning Inspection." Notice the salt and pepper checked pants of the chef and his cleaver knife tucked into his belt. The maid wears a pretty yellow apron, blue necklace and yellow hoop earrings. Retains the manufacturer sticker "Original J B M Design." This is 75% cotton and 25% linen. Artist: Zito. Price range: $22

The cook is rolling out cookie dough as she spies the young man reaching in the window sneaking a few fresh from the oven cookies. She wears blue earrings and matching dotted apron and scarf. Note her orange striped socks and blue shoes. The owner of this towel added colorful hand done crochet work to each end. Price range: $28

Dutch couple. The artist has used many bright colors and decorated the border with beautiful plates, tea cups, and bowls painted with a floral design. Price range: $15

Butler and housemaid. The housemaid holds a feather duster and wears a lacy apron with apple motif. Price range: $15

131

Sweet little house maid carrying a tray with coffee pot and cream. Flowers in flower pots and a corner of the sun is shining through a curtained window. The maid's apron reads "Good Morning." Note her cherubic face and rosy cheeks. Broderie Creations. Manufacturer: A R. Rosenthal & Co. Inc. Price range: $22

Broderie Creations linens can be found in many different designs with their most popular cloths their figural linens. These show ladies and gentlemen or boys and girls, many of them designed with rosy red cheeks, plump rounded bodies and long dark eye lashes. Their designs often show colorful oversized teapots, anthropomorphic vegetables and kitchenware with smiling faces and cute animals done with many details and bright color combinations. Florals, kittens, butlers and maids are among the collectors favorites with polka dots, flowers and ribbons incorporated into many of their designs. They produced kitchen linens including tablecloths and towels, fabricated from cotton, linen and a spun rayon with cotton blend. Manufacturer: A. R. Rosenthal & Co. Inc. Price range: $22

This towel goes with the "Good Morning" towel, with this maid's apron saying "Good Night." Instead of carrying a tray of coffee the tray holds a teapot of calming tea and a lit candle. Broderie Creations. Manufacturer: A. R. Rosenthal & Co. Inc. Price range: $22

A colorful and comical scene showing a startled maid with a spilled cup of coffee. This is a large design with the figure measuring 8 x 10 inches. A Progress Creation. Manufacturer: Tobin, Sporn & Glaser, Inc. New York. Price range: $18

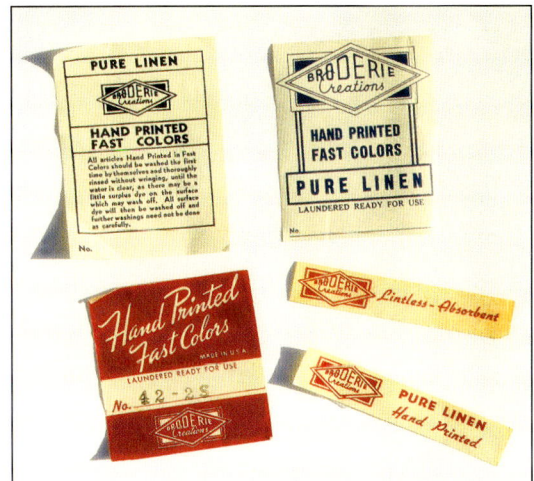

Broderie towel paper tags.

House maid doing canned goods inventory. Oversized cans including beets, figs and plums. Price range: $15

Wash lady. Housewife hanging laundry on the line. Red long johns, yellow towel, and yellow and blue polka dotted pantaloons hang on the line. Yellow puppy with red sock in his mouth, helping out. Price range: $15

Lady with vegetable figure hanging her lingerie on the line. Big red bow in her hair and she carries a basket of linens. Red and blue ribbons interwoven through the lace of her pantaloons, bustier and apron. Note the unusual blue wing-shaped sleeves of her blouse. Price range: $22

1940s, mother and daughter in the kitchen drying the dishes. Top half of towel has oversized cup and saucer, plates, silverware, polka dot tea pot and a sleek martini glass. Hadson. Manufacturer: Carolina Mfg. Price range: $22

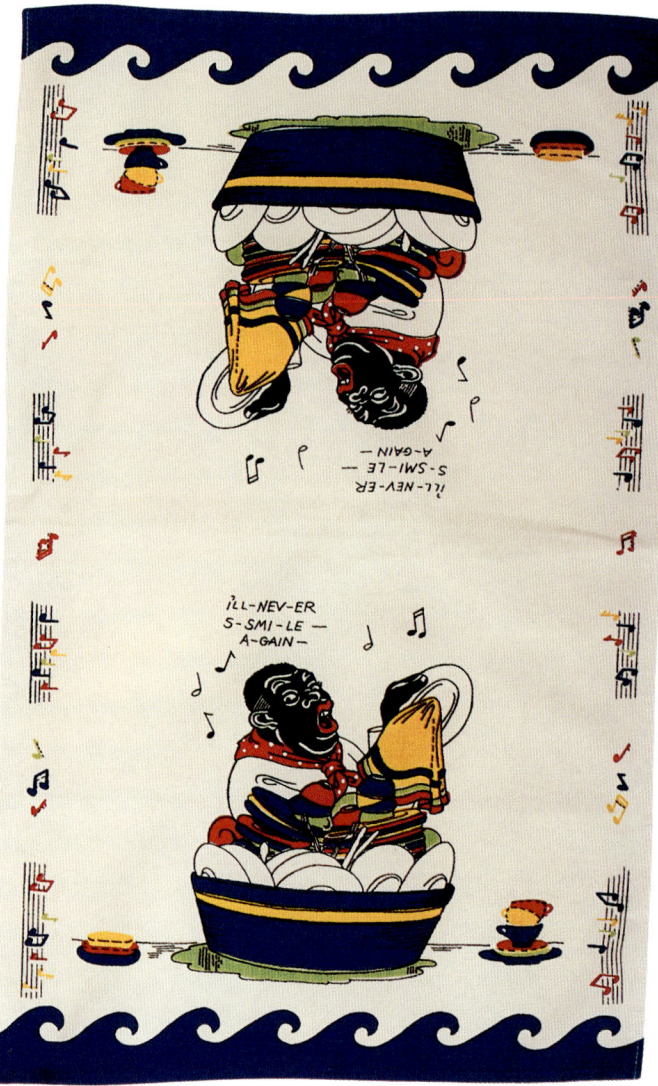

This gentleman eyes the large bucket of dirty dishes and sings "I'll never smile again." The dishes and dish cloth are painted in bright yellow, red, and blue, and the sides are decorated with musical notes. Price range: $25

Wedded Bliss

Beautiful señorita sits in the window while an admirer sings and plays music for her. Sara Jane print. Price range: $18

Wedding day. Happy groom winks at his wife as he carries her over the threshold. Pictures of mother and father grace the walls, and obedient Scottie dog waits at the door. Price range: $15

Wedding scene with bride and groom cutting the cake. The bride has a shy look on her face while the groom has a look of "what did I just do?!" Note the yellow tablecloth with floral garlands. JBM Original Creation. Price range: $15

The housewife puts the apple pie out to cool while her husband looks hungrily on. Note the detailing on this towel with the brick background, green shutters, red checked curtains trimmed in lace, with begonias and morning glories climbing from the window box. Price range: $15

Husband hard at work in the kitchen while the wife relaxes on the couch reading a fashion magazine. It is past 6:00 and dinner still isn't ready but he is doing his best as we can see from the look of serious concentration on his face. Price range: $15

The man of the house has been relegated to doing dishes. Here he stands with dreams of a brand new "automatic dishwasher" as a gift to himself. Blue polka dotted background, yellow checked floor and old style refrigerator. Price range: $15

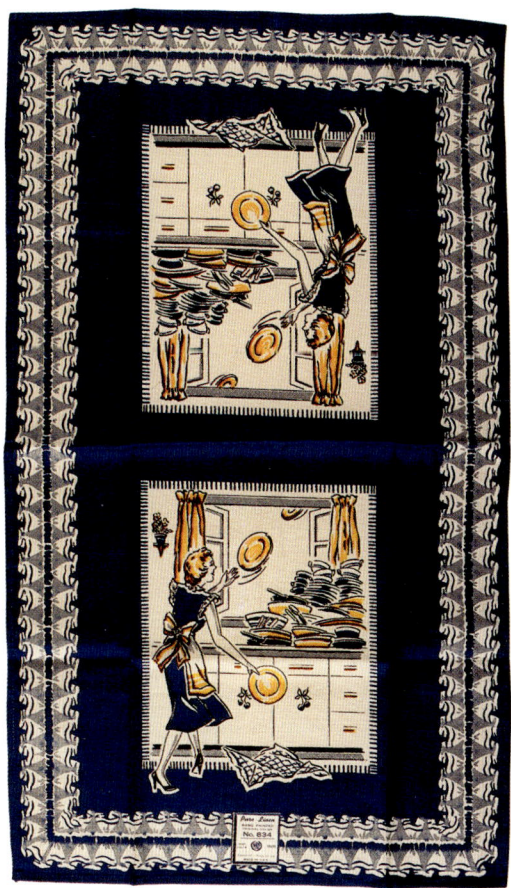

A sink full of dirty dishes and a housewife happily tossing them out the window. Price range: $15

Mom is playing canasta with the girls while dad has charge of the baby. Baby in high chair spilling food and happy Scottie dog at dad's feet. Price range: $15

Affectionate husband and wife with soup boiling over on the stove. Hadson. Manufacturer: Caroline Mfg. Price range: $18

Mom's Crying Towel. This housewife has a lot on her mind and she is letting it go. She airs her disappointments such as "You never say I look pretty!" Price range: $15

Pop's Crying Towel. Here a number of different "Pops'" have their say including "money don't grow on trees you know!" and "if talk was music my wife would be a brass band!" These mom and pop towels were sold in Sears, Roebuck catalogs. Price range: $15

Sears 1957 catalog showing the Mom's and Pop's crying towels. Their description reads "Here is a clever gift idea! Bleached cotton towels with a bright hand-screen printed multicolor pattern of basic household complaints. Size 18 x 27 inches. 2-piece set 92 cents."

An army scene with a bugler playing reveille and a young soldier awakes to the smell of fresh coffee. Sergeant stripes line the border. Price range: $15

Family scene showing husband just home from the office exchanging a kiss with his wife. Children, a kitten and a Scottie dog with big red bow. Hadson. Manufacturer: Carolina Mfg.

Smiling Army cook holding a steaming bowl of soup. Airplanes line the towel border. Retains the original store label from "Timothy Smith Co." and was priced at 29 cents. Broderie Creations. Manufacturer: A. R. Rosenthal and Co. Price range: $30

Smiling mother and daughter admiring a cherry topped cake. Note the little mouse-like figure on the cake. Hadson. Manufacturer: Carolina Mfg. Price range: $18

Charming towel with girl and boy in three different scenes: holding hands and dancing, dancing arm in arm, and sitting together on a flower covered bench. Hadson. Manufacturer: Carolina Mfg. Price range: $15

Young lovers kissing on a park bench with a firecracker ready to go off under their seat. Mischievous little boy with an innocent look on his face walks away. Unusual design on other end shows a child sliding down a banister, a pillow, musical notes and a Pinocchio like figure. Hadson. Manufacturer: Carolina Mfg. Price range: $18

Young couple visiting under the tree with sheep and hay barn in the background. Manufacturer: Hadson. Price range: $15

Childhood

Children

Brightly colored towel with Dutch children surrounded by fields of tulips with fluffy clouds on a blue sky. The little boy carries a rake, the girl holds a water can and we see a sailboat and windmill in the background. This retains the original store tag from The Bailey Company, Cleveland, Ohio, and has an OPA price of 79 cents. Price range: $15

Organ grinder and monkey. As with all Prismacolor towels the colors on this are very bright. The monkey accepts tips in his cup and children dance together to the organ music. The border all around shows children riding carousel horses, playing with balloons and eating ice cream cones. G W Prismacolor. Manufacturer: Grossman and Weissman. Price range: $20

Colorful carousel with children. The sides are decorated with jack-in-the box, balloons, stuffed toys and piggy banks. G W Prismacolor. Manufacturer: Grossman and Weissman. Price range: $18

Sweet little girls doing their daily chores. One holds a broom and sweeps, one stirring bowl, one with wash board scrubbing clothes and one irons. This group is framed by a circle of small flowers. They all have red hair and wear yellow socks with black shoes, each pair of shoes slightly different. They all wear aprons and the little cook wears a chefs hat while the sweeper has her hair tied up in a yellow polka dot scarf. Price range: $15

This little boy appears none too happy about having to wash the dishes. He has an embarrassed look to his face as his friends peer through the window and laugh at him. Note the flowery apron the boy wears and his untied shoes and yellow socks. It seems he had put his football helmet on with plans to play football with his pals when mother decided it was his turn to do dishes. Sides are lined with footballs, helmets and speakers. Price range: $20

Children playing in the sand pile have made a tunnel for their train to go through. Price range: $15

A different design on each end with both framed in hearts. One shows a green haired boy climbing a tree with an owl looking on while the other shows the boy sitting on the ground eating an apple. Hadson. Manufacturer: Carolina Mfg. Price range: $15

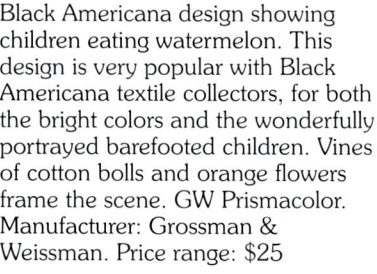

Children on a stroll. He carries a bouquet of flowers and she hold a parasol and small purse. Price range: $15

Black Americana design showing children eating watermelon. This design is very popular with Black Americana textile collectors, for both the bright colors and the wonderfully portrayed barefooted children. Vines of cotton bolls and orange flowers frame the scene. GW Prismacolor. Manufacturer: Grossman & Weissman. Price range: $25

Two children holding a floral wreath and dancing together. The sides are decorated with fans, flowers, bells and accordions. The girl has pink ribbons in her pigtails and wears a lacy petticoat and pantaloons. Hadson. Manufacturer: Carolina Mfg. Price range: $15

Look Ma, No Hands. Little prankster showing off with a stack of dishes on his head, and his distraught mother looking on. Coffee cups border the towel and mothers skirt has a sheer ruffle stitched on. Imperial Creations. Price range: $15

Hadson paper tag

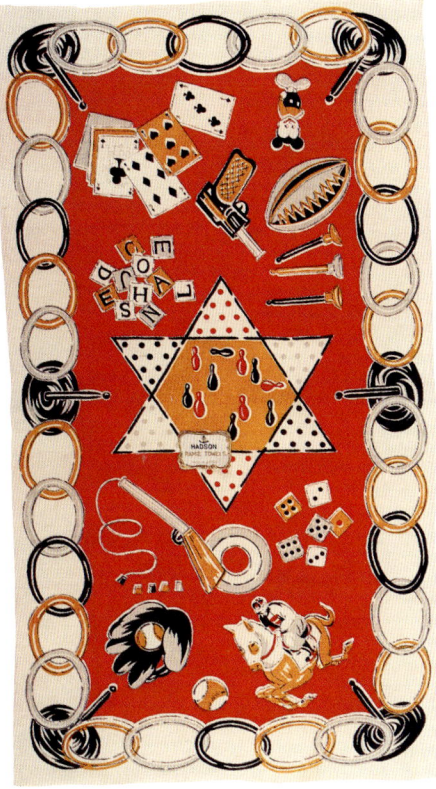

Mammy and child with basket of cotton. A shack and red fence decorate the background with flowers and cotton bolls framing the scene. Startex. Manufacturer: Spartan Mills. Price range: $22

Games motif on this towel with pop gun, dice, baseball glove, man on race horse, dart board, game cards and more. Notice the sMickey Mouse-like figure in the corner. Hadson. Manufacturer: Carolina Mfg. Price range: $18

Two children next to a cart full of potted flowers. The fancy umbrella and the little girls dress are edged in cheerful yellow ruffles. Imperial Creations. Price range: $15

Nursery Rhymes

Many Tobin, Sporn & Glaser stickers and paper tags were imprinted with the company initials, "T S & G."

Old Mother Hubbard towel depicting Old Mother Hubbard at her kitchen cabinet with her dog sitting up asking for a treat. Note the clock on the wall at 2:00 and Mother Hubbard's cane and her shawl around her shoulders. Price range: $18

Little Tommy Tucker. This towel shows a little boy with empty plate in his hands singing. Reads "Little Tommy Tucker Sing For your Supper." Side scenes show barns, row crops, corn and radishes. Top of towel shows a glass of milk and a slice of bread. Ends are decorated with flowery dishes and glass salt and pepper shakers. This is a very charming and detailed towel. Note the stand of hollyhocks behind Tommy, and the details of rabbits on the bread plate. This retains the original "Progress Creation" sticker. Manufacturer: Tobin, Sporn and Glaser. Price range: $20

Pat-A-Cake. Nursery rhyme towel showing the village baker carrying a basket of pastries. He watches the children as they play "pat- a- cake." The boy wears a hat with a feather in it and the girl wears a blue bonnet tied with a red bow. Note the snappy bright yellow and red shoes of the baker and his blue and white striped apron. Price range: $18

Another in the Nursery Rhymes series of towels this is the Queen of Hearts. Red haired queen with rolling pin and jam making jam tarts. Little girl watching from a green trimmed window. Rolling pins, hearts and jam tarts line the sides of the cloth. Note the queens apron with hearts and the heart cut out design of the bench. Price range: $18

Mistress Mary walking along a flowery cottage path with fluffy clouds in the background. She wears a dirndl dress and apron and carries a red watering can. Price range: $18

Little Bo-Peep has lost her sheep. Design showing a sad Bo-Peep, wooden gates, orange flowers and brown sheep. Price range: $18

Circus

Circus theme with happy clown face. He wears a carrot in his hat, and circus big top tents border all around. Price range: $15

Happy clowns with star crossed eyes. Price range: $15

At the circus with the lion tamer, elephant, giraffe and big top tents. Price range: $15

Woman holding bunch of balloons and a basket of yarn by her side. Confetti, ribbons and balloons line the sides. G W Prismacolor. Manufacturer: Grossman & Weissman. Price range: $15

Gentleman sitting on a box and holding a shiny group of balloons. This design is a Royal Doulton character figure called "Balloon Man" designed by Leslie Harradine in 1940. G W Prismacolor. Manufacturer: Grossman & Weissman. Price range: $15

A day at the circus with a clown playing an accordion, a steaming train engine and an elephant spraying himself with water. Price range: $15

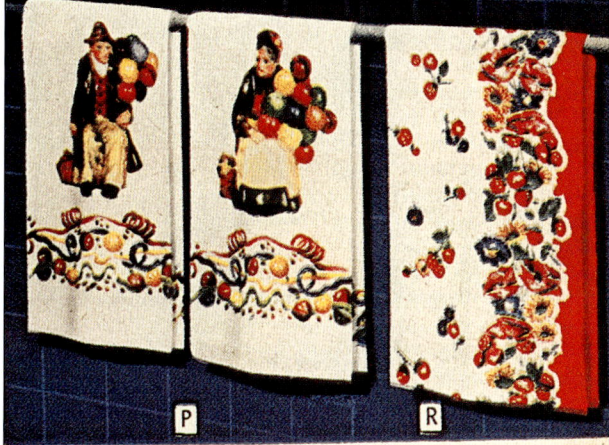

Sears, Roebuck and Co. catalog 1947. These 16 x 28 inch towels were priced at 55 cents each. "The ever popular Balloon Lady and Balloon Man are printed in gay multicolor on good quality cotton twill. The attractive towels with their clever wash-fast designs are ideal for inexpensive gifts or prizes."

Bath Sets & Pillows

This is a French poodle design with a bath towel, two guest towels and two wash cloths. Eiffel towel, flowers and a fancy poodle with a top hat and cane. Manufacturer: Lila Lou. Price range: $25

His and Hers bath towel set with pink roses, wash cloths and bow. Price range: $25

Montgomery Ward & Co. Fall and Winter 1929-1930 catalog. Turkish towel sets priced at 79 cents for a three piece boxed set of one 17 x 34 inch towel with two 12 x 12 inch washcloths. A boxed set of three for $1.00 had a slightly larger towel of 21 x 40 inches. "Popular fast colored Turkish towels, charming and practical."

This Turkish bath towel set dates to the 1930s. The box cover for this set is shown next. Manufacturer: Martex. Price range: $25

Label for Martex bath set

Cannon towel advertisement from 1934 Collier's magazine showing housewives hanging their Cannon towels on the line to dry.

Many of the boxes used for these sets were beautiful unto themselves, such as this box cover with a painting of a lovely woman.

151

Cannon towel gift set. These are Cannon towels that were designed and packaged as a gift set by the J. F. Zucker Company. This was a "Fashion of the day" gift set which was a brand of sets that were designed with themes depicting styles, fashions or ideas popular at that time. This set shows "My Fair Lady" and "Most Happy Fella" towels which the paper tag states were "inspired by the Broadway hit plays". Since we know Fashion of the day gift sets designed only current themes we can date these towels to the Spring of 1956. The musical show "My Fair Lady" opened on Broadway on March 15, 1956 and starred Rex Harrison and Julie Andrews. The most happy fella opened on May 3, 1956 at the Imperial Theatre and starred Robert Weede, Jo Sullivan, and Art Lund. Price range: $20

Pillows are a wonderful way to make use of vintage towels that are too damaged for use or display. A talented seamstress fabricated this beautiful pillow from a vintage 1950's floral towel, combined checks, lace and ruffle to finish and voila, a perfect accent piece for a flowery cottage décor. Price range: $30

A wonderful gift for the Black Americana collector, this pillow combines a colorful mammy towel with fabric in stripes, checks and polka dots and an all around trim of white chenille pom poms. Price range: $35

Cleaning and Storage

This towel is covered with different containers of food and cleaning products. Notice how they copied containers of well-known items and then changed one letter in the name. Yellow box of Suz, instead of Duz, can of Cisco, instead of Crisco etc. Very colorful and detailed towel. Hadson. Manufacturer: Carolina Mfg. Made in Japan. Price range: $18

First Rinse It

After obtaining a stained or soiled linen, give it a thorough rinsing in clean water before laundering it. This will rinse away excessive dirt so if you plan to soak the cloth it will not be soaking in dirty water.

Glass Towel. This towel shows many different types of glassware such as champagne and wine glasses along with various shaped vases. Price range: $15

Then Wash It

Choose your favorite detergent. I use Oxy Prime for laundering and Oxy Boost for destaining as I have found these products to do an excellent job of whitening and destaining old linens. However, linens containing rayon, silk fibers, or metallic accents can be damaged by Oxy products so a better detergent choice for these items would be Biz. Using the sink or a wash bucket, work up a good soapy mixture and gently swish the item through the water, let it soak, then swish several more times to release any soil. Rinse thoroughly several times until the water runs clean. If there are still noticeable stains after this first cleaning, spot treat the stains, then soak for two hours in detergent. Always rinse repeatedly until the water runs clean.

Pat these items dry between towels and lay flat to dry or line dry on a calm, not windy, day.

Stubborn stains can sometimes be lightened by placing the towel, while still damp, on green grass outdoors on a sunny day. This will also brighten

Laundry hanging on the line with the towels spelling out the words "tea towel." Price range: $21

whites and refresh old linen. The added benefit to this method is the towel will now have that wonderful fresh grassy scent.

I do not recommend chlorine bleach on vintage linens. I have been able to remove or lighten stains using alternative, gentler methods. Reserve bleach for your last choice when other treatments do not work and make sure the item is structurally strong, not fragile. Used often, bleach can damage the fibers and fade colors. Remember, colorfast does not mean un-fadeable.

Do not "over treat" your vintage towels. In other words, use the gentlest treatment possible to avoid further damage and be reasonable in your expectations for the end results. I generally do no more than two overnight soaks on an item.

Storage

Do not store linens in direct sunlight, as sunlight will cause colors to fade.

Do not store your linens directly on raw or treated wood shelves as the acid and chemicals can damage the textile, causing discoloration to the fabric. Line your shelves with any of the following:

    Acid-free tissue paper
    White pure cotton towels
    White pure cotton sheets

If stored in a very dusty environment layer the same protective cloth on top of your linens.

This is a gift boxed days of the week towel set in terrycloth. There are only six towels here for, as the attached tag says, "Sunday Day Off No Work". Price range: $25

Mangle Irons

I use an Ironrite mangle iron for pressing. Mangle irons are wonderful old machines that do a beautiful job of pressing. One can press a great number of articles in a short time using one, and the end result is a crisp, perfectly ironed item. Those of us who use mangle irons would now find it very difficult to go back to a hand iron.

Flea markets are a good place to search for a mangle iron, and one can find not just the Ironrite brand, but also Sears, General Electric, and others. Many have remained unused for many years, stored away in mother's or grandmother's basement, and are now finding their way out, to be sold in garage sales. The are often sold quite cheaply by home owners happy to get that big machine out of the way.

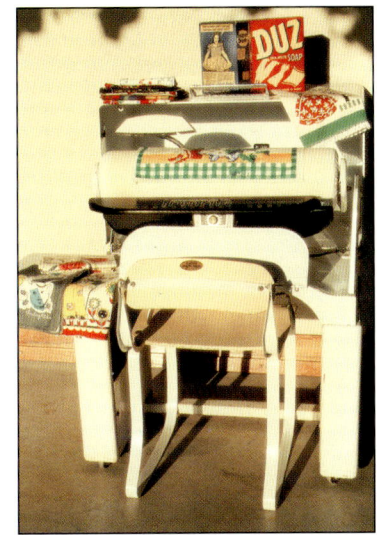

Ironrite mangle iron.

Glossary

Absorbent Finish – A chemical treatment of fabrics to enable them to absorb water more readily.

Art Linen – A plain linen used for embroidery. It is woven with even threads that are especially good for needlework. Used for lunch cloths, napkins, and embroidery crash.

Beach Cloth – Lightweight, cotton warp and mohair filling or all cotton in imitate linen crash. For summer clothing, nurses' uniforms, draperies, table scarves.

Birdseye – Cotton or linen cloth with a small geometric pattern that has a center dot resembling a bird's eye. Woven on a dobby loom, the filling yarns are heavier and loosely twisted to make the material more absorbent. Used for linen or cotton towels and runners. Also a type of pique with characteristic diamond design.

Bleaching – Necessary process to remove the natural and artificial impurities in fabrics to obtain clear whites for even dyeing and printing. This process increased the fabric's affinity for dyestuffs. Different chemicals are used for different fabrics, but after washing or cleaning, the natural yellowish color of the fiber may slowly return. Some linens are "grass bleached"...whitened by exposure to the sun, air and moisture. This process is slower.

Broad Goods – Fabrics woven 18 inches or more in width.

Cambric – Soft, white, closely woven cotton fabric calendered on right side with slight gloss. Used for underwear, aprons, shirts, and handkerchiefs. Originally made in Cambrai, France, of linen and used for church embroidery and table linen.

Colorfast – A term used to describe fabrics of sufficient color retention so that no noticeable change in shade takes place during the normal life of the garment. Strictly speaking, no fabric is "colorfast". In buying fabrics, make sure they are fast to the particular color hazard they will encounter.

Completely Washable Fabric – A fabric washable by machine in water hot enough to clean the fabric efficiently (160 in the tub).

Construction – The method by which a textile cloth is fabricated. It may be woven, knitted, felted, bonded, braided or laminated.

Cotton – Soft fiber obtained from the seedpod of the cotton plant. Was first known in India about 3000 B.C., and was considered very rare and precious. Today it is one of America's greatest crops, and is spun into yarn and thread, woven and knitted into fabrics. Different types of cotton have different fiber lengths. Usually, the longer the fiber, the better the quality of cotton.

Crash – A course fabric having a rough irregular surface obtained by weaving thick uneven yarns. Usually cotton or linen, sometimes spun rayon or blends. Made in various weights, and used for dresses, draperies, table linens. Softer weave woolen crash used widely for men and women's suitings, draperies.

Damask – Firm, glossy Jacquard patterned fabric first brought to the Western world by Marco Polo in the 13th century. Damascus was the center of fabric trade between the East and West; hence the name. Damask is similar to brocade but flatter and reversible. It may be linen, cotton, rayon, silk, or a combination of fibers. Used for tablecloths, napkins, draperies, and upholstery.

Detergent – A cleansing agent or solvent. The term originally applied to soap and certain water softeners and soap savers. Now the term applies to new washing products call "synthetic detergents", so named to distinguish them from soaps.

Dyeing – A process of coloring fibers or fabrics with either natural or synthetic dyes. Dyes differ in their resistance to sunlight, perspiration, washing, gas, alkali, dust, etc., their effectiveness on different fibers, and their reaction to cleaning agents, their solubility and method of application.

Fabric (Textile) – A cloth formed of fibers or yarns, either by knitting, weaving, braiding, felting, bonding, or laminating.

Fiber (Textile) – The basic unit used in the fabrication of textile yarn and fabrics.

Finish – A general term covering treatment of a fabric to give a desired surface effect such as napping, calendaring, embossing, lacquering, etc. Some finishes add luster, others give a muted dull effect. Special finishes can be applied to make a fabric waterproof or wrinkle resistant. A finish often contributes much to the "feel" of a fabric.

Flax – Fibers of the flax plant. Spun into linen yarns and then woven into linen fabrics.

Glass Toweling – Fabric of plain cotton or linen or combinations of these fibers with rayon, with checks or color on white ground. Used for drying glasses.

Grass Bleaching – The bleaching of cotton or linen by spreading it on the grass and exposing it to light and air. This is a slower process than chemical bleaching.

Grey Goods – Also spelled greige. They are cloths, irrespective of color, as they come from the loom without having received any wet or dry finishing. Cotton, rayon and acetate grey good are taken by the converter to be dyed, printed and finished as desired for the end use. In the silk and rayon trades, these fabrics are often called greige goods.

Hand – Refers to the "feel" of a fabric involving such physical properties as flexibility, compressibility, and resilience.

Heavy-Duty Soap – A pure and mild cleansing agent that has special alkalies added to improve its cleaning power.

Heavy-Duty Synthetic Detergent – A cleansing agent that has a builder added for improved cleaning power. A suds-making ingredient is added primarily for use in automatic washers.

Huck – A toweling fabric with a honeycombed surface made by using heavy filling yarns in dobby weave. Have excellent absorbent qualities. Made in either linen or cotton, or a mixture of both, In a mixture it is called a "union" towel. Full name is huckaback.

Launder-Proof – Fabrics and garments which have been laboratory-tested to withstand laundering without losing color or shrinking under normal washing conditions and length of time. This term can only be applied to fabrics that have been so tested.

Laundry-Tested And Approved Seal – A seal awarded by the American Institute of Laundering to guide the public in the purchase of washable merchandise that has all the characteristics of launderability – color fastness to washing, sun, gas, and perspiration; adequate tensile strength; dimensional stability; satisfactory construction.

Linen – Strong lustrous yarn or fabric of smooth-surfaced flax fibers. Can be either plain weave or a Jacquard weave for table damask. Used for wearing apparel, household articles, fancy work.

Mercerizing – A treatment for cottons using caustic soda at low temperature, which makes cotton stronger, more lustrous, more absorbent and more susceptible to dye. Named for its originator John Mercer.

Print - General term for fabric with design from dyes applied by engraved rollers, wood blocks or screens.

Resist Print – The principle used in batik dyeing. Substances that will resist dye are applied to a fabric in designs, and then the fabric is dipped in dye. Then the "resist" is removed.

Screen Print – Method similar to a stencil. Background of designs is painted on screen (bolting cloth) with paste, and dye is printed through exposed fabric. Separate screens may be used for different colors.

Stencil Print – A type of resist printing. Portions of the design to be resisted are covered with paper or metal so those parts do not take dye.

Wedgwood Print – Print of white design on colored ground similar to the effects of Wedgwood china.

Print Cloth – Plain weave cloth with yarn counts from 30s to 40s. Fabric similar to sheeting from averaging finer yarns and construction.

Ramie – A fiber similar to flax, obtained from stalk of plant grown in China, United States, and Japan.

Selvage or Selvedge – The outer reinforced edge of a cloth woven from special yarns.

Sizing – 1. A finishing process in which a substance such as wax, glue, casein or clay is added to yarn and cloth to give it additional strength, stiffness, smoothness or weight. 2. Also the determining of the count or yarn number of a yarn.

Soap – A cleansing agent produced by the action of caustic soda and a fat. Neutral soap has no free alkali.

Sunfast – Dyed fabrics, which will not fade under normal exposure to sunlight, or under standard tests with the Fade-Ometer. Since no fabric is absolutely "sunfast", term is somewhat misleading. "Sun resistant" is preferred.

Terry – Cotton fabric covered with loops on one or both sides, made by using two sets of warp threads and one set of filling threads. During the weaving process, one set of the warp threads is held tight, the other is left loose to form the loops. It is extremely water absorbent, and is used primarily for bath towels and beach robes. Named from the French verb meaning to pull out.

Textile – A fabric that has been woven, knitted, felted, bonded, braided, crocheted, or knotted. Also material suitable for forming fabrics.

Toweling – Materials for towels especially those woven in long pieces, bought by the yard and hand-hemmed by the purchaser. Includes such fabrics as crash, birdseye, damask, honeycomb, huck, twill and terry.

Vegetable Fibers – All textile fibers of vegetable original such as cotton, kapok, jute, ramie, and flax.

Waffle Cloth – Fabric with a characteristic honeycomb weave. When made in cotton, it is called waffle pique. Used for coatings, draperies, dresses, toweling. Same as Honeycomb Cloth.

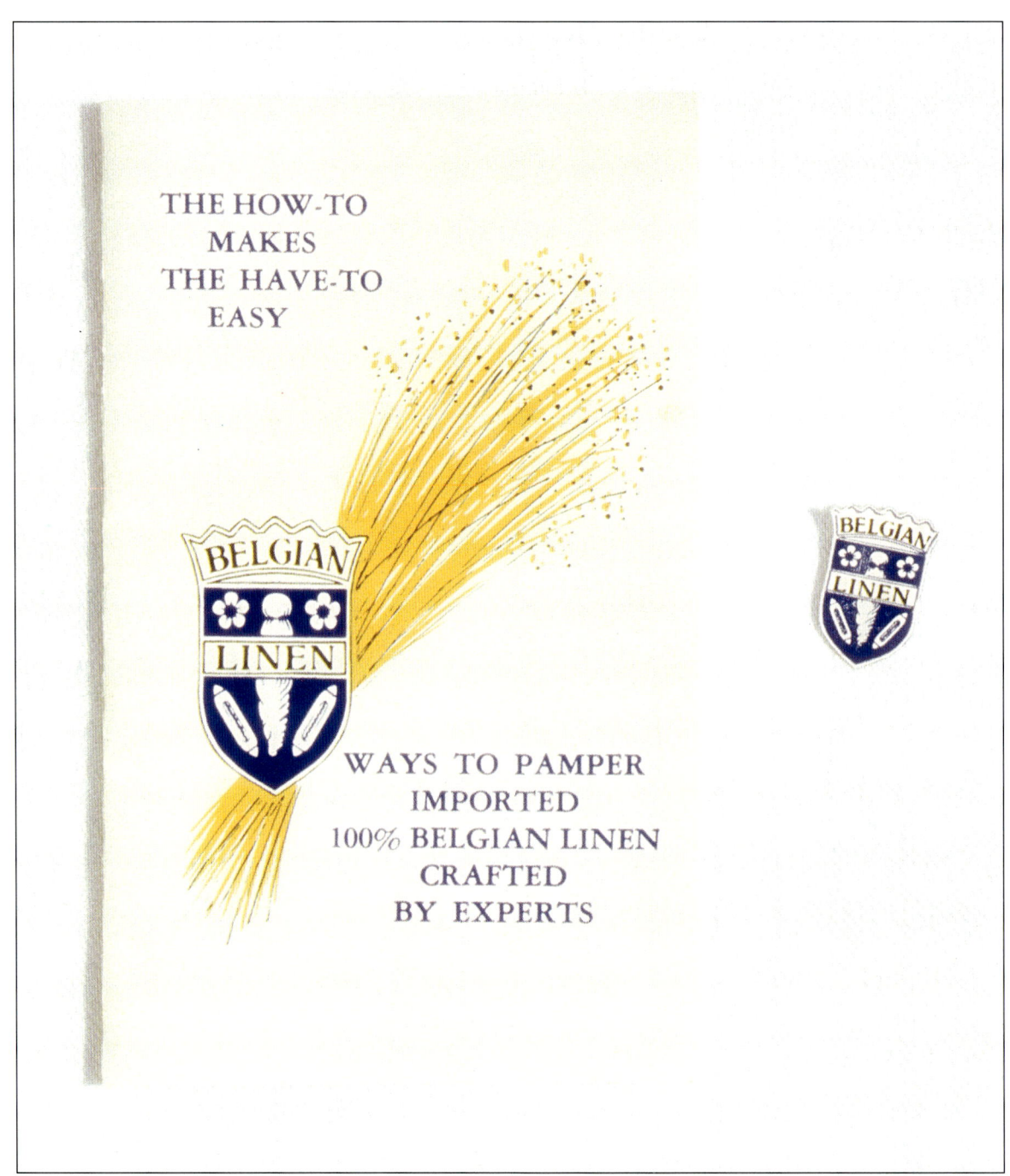

Belgian Linen tag. Vintage towels fabricated from pure Belgian linen can often be found with the Belgian Linen Association Shield as shown here. This shield assured the customer that they were purchasing the finest quality linen. In 1981 the Belgian Linen Association joined forces with other Western European linen producers which now work under the umbrella of Masters of Linen. Masters of Linen is the quality identity label for European linen of quality.

Bibliography

Ahern, Eleanor. *The Way We Wash Our Clothes.* New York. M. Barrows & Company. 1941.

Corbman, Dr. Bernard. *Textiles: Fiber To Fabric.* New York: McGraw-Hill Book Company 1975.

Dan River Mills, Inc., 1964. *A Dictionary of Textile Terms,* 9th Edition. Danville, Virginia.

Glasell, Pamela. *Collectors Guide to Vintage Tablecloths.* Atglen, Pennsylvania: Schiffer Publishing, Ltd. 2002.

Scofield, Elizabeth and Zalamea, Peggy. *Fun Linens & Handkerchiefs of the 20th Century.* Atglen, Pennsylvania: Schiffer Publishing, Ltd. 2002.

Temple, Mary Beth. *Rescuing Vintage Textiles.* Haworth, New Jersey: St. Johann Press, 2000.

Which toweling shall I buy?

Linen is the strongest, toughest of all vegetable fibers. In general, Linen threads are thicker than Cotton, so there are fewer to the square inch.

Because of the natural properties of Linen, it does not lint as readily as Cotton. Also, has the power of holding moisture without losing its firm body.

Part Linen combines Linen with Cotton in varying percentages, and generally the more Linen a towel contains the more satisfactory you will find it.

Bleaching — quality for quality Unbleached is stronger, wears longer, costs less, but Bleached is softer and more readily absorbent.

Index

Artmark, 101
Belgian Linen Asoc., 158
Bernard Ulmann, 15
Broderie, 27-28, 32, 34, 49, 77, 115-116, 126, 132, 139
Bucilla, 15-17, 61, 68, 85, 130
California Hand Prints, 98
Cannon, 19, 21-24, 40, 151-152
Carolina Mfg., 24.
don, 74
Doris Duffee, 18
Eaton, see Novelty, see Technicolor Print.
Elsie the cow, 75
Exclusive, 124
Fallani & Cohn, 18, 38-39, 90
Fieldcrest, 19
G W Prismacolor, 7, 52, 99, 141-142, 144, 149
Garden State House of Prints, 126
Hadson, 24, 33, 45, 50, 96, 101, 103, 111, 116, 125-127, 134, 137, 139-140, 143-145, 153
Hardycraft, 108
Hedaya, 35-36, 81
Imperial Creations, 111, 120-122, 125, 144-145
J.P. Stevens, 12-13, 72, 90
JBM Original Creation, 128, 130, 135
JS&S, see Sultan, Joseph
Kay Dee Handprints, 112
Keefe, Tammis, 87, 90
Lamb, Tom, 27, 88
Leacock and Company, 28, 31, 65, 72, 108, 110
Liberace, 112
Lila Lou, 150
Long, Lois, 35, 36
Lyons, Ruth, Index.
Martex, 8-12, 45-46, 67, 151
Martha, 79, 108, 110
Meier, C.P. 107
Morrow, Tom, 72
Neumann, Vera, see Vera

Novelty, 97
OPA, 7
Original Town House Kitchen Decoratives, 36
Orr, Ann, 10, 12
P & S, 30, 72
Paragon Needlecraft Corp., 34, 62, 78
Parisian Prints, 54, 92, 109, 110
Pearson, Fred, 89
Pepperell, 13
Pillowtex, 19
Prints Charming, 74
Progress Creations, 26, 37, 132, 146
Rosenthal, A.R., see Broderie
Sara Jane Print, 102, 135
Sarg, Mary, 106
Silver Dust, 23
Spartan Mills, 14
Springmaid, 25
Startex, 13-14, 26, 35, 39, 52, 82, 84, 95-97, 99, 102, 145, Index
Steiger, Harwood, 104
Sultan, Joseph & Sons, 109
Sunweave Linen Corp., 74

Taylor, Richard, 89
Technicolor Print, 43, 93, 97, 105-106
Thall, Willie, 28
Tobin, Sporn & Glaser, 37
Town & Country Linen Corporation, 44, 78-79, 86, 91
Travis, Luther 18, 38-39, 86
Vera, 64, 67, 70
Victory K & B, 89
Vogart, 29
Weil & Durrse, 14-15, 38, 53, 98
Wert, Robert Darr, 90
Westpoint Stevens, 13
Wilendur, see Weil & Durrse
Wilson, Carrie, 71
Zito, 128, 130
Zito, Virginia, 107

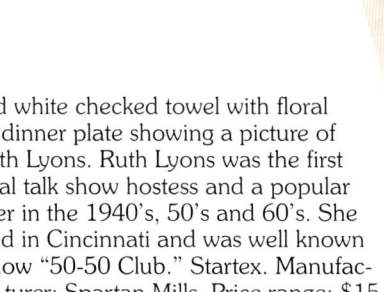

Red and white checked towel with floral edged dinner plate showing a picture of Ruth Lyons. Ruth Lyons was the first national talk show hostess and a popular broadcaster in the 1940's, 50's and 60's. She was based in Cincinnati and was well known for her show "50-50 Club." Startex. Manufacturer: Spartan Mills. Price range: $15